The 175 BeST CaMP GaMeS

A HANDBOOK FOR LEADERS

The 175 BeST CaMP GaMeS

A HANDBOOK FOR LEADERS

Kathleen, Laura & Mary Fraser

With Illustrations by Bernice Lum

The BOSTON
MILLS PRESS

A BOSTON MILLS PRESS BOOK

Copyright © Kathleen, Laura and Mary Fraser, 2009

Published by Boston Mills Press, 2009
132 Main Street, Erin, Ontario, Canada N0B 1T0
Tel: 519-833-2407 • Fax: 519-833-2195
e-mail: books@bostonmillspress.com   www.bostonmillspress.com

In Canada:
Distributed by Firefly Books Ltd.
66 Leek Crescent, Richmond Hill, Ontario, Canada L4B 1H1

In the United States:
Distributed by Firefly Books (U.S.) Inc.
P.O. Box 1338, Ellicott Station, Buffalo, New York, USA 14205

The publisher gratefully acknowledges the financial support for our publishing program by the
Government of Canada through the Book Publishing Industry Development Program (BPIDP).

Library and Archives Canada Cataloguing in Publication

Fraser, Kathleen, 1957-
The 175 best camp games : a handbook for leaders / Kathleen, Laura & Mary Fraser ;
with illustrations by Bernice Lum.

Includes bibliographical references and index.
ISBN-13: 978-1-55046-505-1 (pbk.)   ISBN-13: 978-1-55046-516-7 (bound)
ISBN-10: 1-55046-505-8 (pbk.)   ISBN-10: 1-55046-516-3 (bound)

1. Group games. 2. Outdoor games. 3. Indoor games. I. Fraser, Laura, 1985-
II. Fraser, Mary, 1983- III. Lum, Bernice IV. Title. V. Title: One hundred
seventy-five best camp games.

GV1203.F73 2009   790.1'5   C2009-902035-1

Publisher Cataloging-in-Publication Data (U.S.)

Fraser, Kathleen, 1957-
The 175 best camp games : a handbook for leaders / Kathleen, Laura & Mary Fraser ;
with illustrations by Bernice Lum.
[160] p. : col. ill. ; cm.
Includes bibliographical references and index.
Summary: An illustrated handbook of outdoor and indoor games for camp counselors, group leaders,
teachers, recreation program leaders and parents to play with children and young adults at camp,
school, home and elsewhere. Includes games, leadership activities, ideas for modifying games for abilities,
advice on how to run camp programs and include all participants, and many more tips on making games fair and fun.

ISBN-13: 978-1-55046-505-1 (pbk.)   ISBN-13: 978-1-55046-516-7 (bound)
ISBN-10: 1-55046-505-8 (pbk.)   ISBN-10: 1-55046-516-3 (bound)

1. Games for campers. 2. Outdoor games. 3. Indoor games.
I. Fraser, Laura, 1985- . II. Fraser, Mary, 1983- . III. Lum, Bernice. IV. One hundred seventy-five best camp games. V. Title.

790.15 dc22   GV1202.C36F737 2009

Design by Chris McCorkindale and Sue Breen, McCorkindale Advertising & Design
Illustrations by Bernice Lum
Edited by Kathleen Fraser
Printed in China

To contact the authors, email bestcampgames@gmail.com

For Sally and Cam

CONTENTS

Get Them Moving

TIPS FOR LEADERS

Introduction

WE BEGAN AS KIDS, eager to play and even more eager to fit in. We wore old sneakers and hats that made our ears stick out. We thought that our camp in a park in the suburbs was pretty close to being in the wilderness. We thought our counselors were the bee's knees, especially when bees stung our knees and we needed ice packs and a hug.

We returned later as leaders, eager to help new campers make friends and have fun. We wore old sneakers and hats that made our ears stick out. We sometimes wished that our camp in a park in the suburbs was a sleep-away camp in the wilderness, but we were glad when we got to go home at the end of the day. We thought our campers were amazing and enthusiastic kids, even though they sometimes drove us a little crazy. We were proud when we could give them ice packs or a hug, but were even more proud when we handed the kids back to their parents, knowing that each child had enjoyed his or her day and felt like a meaningful part of a team.

Years later, teaching in classrooms, we meet our former campers and feel honored when their 13-year-old brains remember a summer we spent together when they were five and we played camp games.

WHY WE PLAY GAMES

Games are the most useful tool we know in aiding childhood development. They help children develop hand-eye coordination, fine motor skills, listening skills, and the ability to think, respond and strategize. They encourage children to work together as a team to achieve a common goal. They allow children to experience success and failure in a positive and supportive environment. They help children communicate with each other and with adults. They teach children valuable life lessons, such as "if you break a rule, you have to deal with the consequences," or "if you brag about winning the game, nobody will want to play against you next time."

Today, as children's time in front of various "screens" (television, computer, video game) is increasing, it is more and more important to encourage children to play games with other real, live kids. Particularly for children who do not have brothers or sisters, and children who do not live in child-friendly neighborhoods, playing games at camp, at a recreation program, or at school may be the only time that they get to interact socially with other children in their age group without the structure of learning a specific sports drill or vocabulary word.

In addition to the social benefits of game playing, the health benefits of daily physical activity are well documented. Play is extremely important in developing healthy children who will go on to become healthy adults. By getting kids up and moving, we teach them the importance of physical activity in living a healthy and long life.

WHY WE WROTE THIS BOOK

During our collective years as camp counselors and teachers-in-training, we found a great many games books. Some of them included detailed rules for sports; some of them had exhaustive descriptions of pencil and paper games, or card games. Some described games that encouraged pummeling playmates! But none of them seemed to contain what we needed. We needed camp-tested games that would excite even the most seasoned camp veterans. We needed a games book that took into consideration the concerns of today's

recreation programs and addressed issues such as supervision, safety, and inclusion of children of all ages and abilities, including those with special needs or behavioral challenges.

We began cobbling together binders with notes of games we played when visiting other programs, games we saw someone else play or heard someone describe, or games that we had tried before, but had found ways to modify to make them more exciting and engaging for each individual participant.

As we moved from the world of day camps to the world of teaching, we decided we needed to write this book. We needed to take our notes and turn them into a guide for today's camp counselors, youth activity directors, recreational program leaders, counselors-in-training, teachers, coaches, scout and club leaders, parents and anyone else looking for creative group activities that include all participants and require little or no specialized equipment.

HOW TO USE THIS BOOK

Just because the title of the book is *The 175 Best Camp Games* doesn't mean these games are meant only for camps: they can be played in schoolyards, gymnasiums, community centers and backyards year-round. With games for all levels of movement and activity, and games that appeal to a variety of age groups and activities, this book will help you play with just about any group of children.

We have divided the games into five chapters: Break the Ice, Take It Easy, Get Them Moving, Run Them Ragged, and Wet and Wild.

Games in **BREAK THE ICE** work best at the beginning of the program session, as many of them are based on learning each other's names and getting to know each other. These games range in activity level and amount of space required, but none of them will leave your participants exhausted. And although these games are ice-breakers, they can be played throughout the camp session to develop group unity and a team atmosphere. At the end of this chapter we also include some activities especially good for building skills and spirit among leaders and leaders-in-training.

TAKE IT EASY games require only minimal movement. However, they are not necessarily easy or low-energy

or quiet: we don't believe that any game is a quiet game (with the exception of Silent Ball, at page 66). These games are good to play right after an exhausting game of tag, or just after lunch when tummies are full. Most of these games will work well in small spaces. This chapter includes a number of brain games.

GET THEM MOVING games require some movement and physical activity. These games are usually on-your-feet and may require quick bursts of speed to get from one place to another. They generally require a larger playing area than Take It Easy games, but many can still be played inside. We've included relays in this chapter.

RUN THEM RAGGED games are designed to exhaust your participants, to burn off their energy, and to raise heart rates. These games usually require a medium or large space and, though many can be played in gyms, most are more fun outdoors. Many variations of tag are included in this chapter.

Finally, **WET AND WILD** games are played in, around, or with water. Some of them are in-pool games, some can be played in a lake or river, and others use equipment such as buckets of water, sponges or water balloons to get participants wet and cooled off.

Sport Rules

We decided early on not to include rules for the usual team sports games. The rules can be found elsewhere, in books where the focus is on sports. And the truth is, the usual sports games generally don't fit our criteria for being the best camp games.

Additionally, with many children enrolled in sports teams outside of camp or school, we find that playing sports may provide opportunity for star athletes to show off their skills, but often alienates those campers in a recreation environment who either can't afford to play AA soccer or simply choose not to participate in organized sports and don't have the skill level to compete against their more practiced peers.

RAINY DAY GAMES can be played in spaces as small as a tent on wet-weather days. Of course, they can also be played outside when it's dry.

 LARGE GROUP GAMES are best with 15 or more players and can often be played with groups of 30 or more.

 BRAIN GAMES require participants to use their strategizing, memory and problem-solving skills.

 EASY IN, EASY OUT games are games without elimination that participants can easily join or leave without affecting the outcome of the game.

 PLAN-AHEAD GAMES require some advanced planning – for example, filling up water balloons, drawing chalk outlines on the floor or selecting child-appropriate music.

 MAKE-BELIEVE GAMES involve using your imagination: these range from imitating animals all the way to acting out charades.

 EASY-TO-FOLLOW GAMES require limited instructions and limited specialized skill.

 EVERYBODY WINS GAMES involve the entire group playing together and working toward a common goal.

 TEAM-BUILDER GAMES develop teamwork and cooperation and teach children how to compete fairly and leaders-in-training how to work together.

In addition to dividing the games by chapter, we have used several handy icons to help game leaders match their programing needs to the games in the book.

See the key, left, for an explanation of what each icon means.

We also share our camp-tested strategies for keeping play fun, fair and safe. Throughout the book we have included many recommendations and tips on how to play games, encourage participants and structure a camp program. These **TIPS FOR LEADERS** are based on our years of experience, especially at camp but also in school environments, as well as many enjoyable occasions spent comparing notes with other camp counselors, parents and educators.

With each game, you will find a list of required equipment, a recommended number of participants, and a game plan. Many games also include variations and suggestions for modifying games to include more or fewer participants, to increase or decrease the difficulty level, and to include participants with physical, intellectual or developmental disabilities or behavior challenges. These suggestions will help you keep your participants safe, happy and having fun, but leaders should continually monitor the games and activities the group is playing to prevent injured bodies and hurt feelings.

We encourage you to use this book as a starting guide for developing your own recreation program, whether it is in a camp, a school classroom or in your own backyard. Take our games and create your own rules. Make them fit the needs of your program and your participants. Use your imagination to create a new twist on an old classic, or combine the rules of two games to create a new super-game.

And be proud when, at the end of the day, you hear the kids saying how much fun they had playing games with you.

CAUTION You are responsible for the children in your care. We love these games and have played them safely for endless hours, but accidents can happen and mistakes in judgement can have serious consequences. Please use your common sense and informed judgement when trying out any games, and don't be afraid to call to a stop any game that is getting out of control.

Break the Ice

THE MOST NERVE-WRACKING MOMENT between a child and a program leader is almost always the first one. The child is wondering whether the leader is going to be a bully or a bore, or overly enthusiastic or even scary. The leader is wondering whether the child is going to be a bully or a bore, or so enthusiastic that he or she will take over the whole group. Add to that stress all the other children eyeing each other, trying to figure out who will be the teacher's pet, who will steal people's lunches, who is fastest and who is slowest, and who might possibly be friend or foe.

The games in this chapter are intended to defuse all that anxiety: they get leaders and participants working together to learn each other's names and begin working as a team. Children and leaders form icy little bubbles around themselves that protect their egos and keep them safe from teasing or embarrassment. Unfortunately, those bubbles also prevent the children from having fun. The games in this chapter break those icy individual bubbles between people and encourage them to warm up to each other.

My Name Is Aaron and I Like Aardvarks

PLAYERS Fewer than 30

EQUIPMENT None

GAME PLAN Learn everyone's name.

HOW TO PLAY

This is a name game that that requires nothing more than the alphabet to play.

Have the group sit in a circle. Begin the game by asking all the players to think of something that shares the same first letter as their name.

For younger children, you might have to help them with rare first letters such as Q or Y, or you might have to extend the first letter to the first sound (so that Kathy or Cathy could pick cat, carrots, crazy or Kathmandu).

For older children, you can limit items to a particular category, for example, animal, food, adjective or place.

Try to not have two players pick the same item. It doesn't really matter whether or not the child actually likes the thing chosen — the matching is only for memory purposes. After each player has picked an item, the game can begin.

The first person in the circle says his or her name and thing. For example, "My name is Kathy and I like koalas," or "My name is Lizzie and I like lollipops," or "My name is Joanne and I am joyful," or "My name is Herbert and I would go to Halifax."

The person to the left of the first person then says, "That is Herbert and he would go to Halifax. I am Maddy and I would go to Maine."

The next person to the left then says, "That is Herbert and he would go to Halifax. That is Maddy and she would go to Maine. I am Stuart and I would go to Switzerland." The game continues until all the players have had a turn.

While it is impressive when the last player knows everyone's name without making a mistake, it can actually be more fun and more helpful when learning names to make mistakes.

Sometimes, depending on the energy level of the participants, you can go through the circle again so that each player gets a shot at remembering everyone's name.

VARIATIONS

For children with poor memory skills, have them repeat what their teammates say immediately afterward, rather than having them remember the whole group all at once.

MODIFICATIONS

Have players make a funny face, do a silly dance, or sing their name. This works equally well for expressive, out-of-the-box players and players who aren't confident speaking in front of others.

How to Start Games

Before starting any game, clarify the boundaries and any particular safety expectations for that game. For example, you might decide that you are playing this version of Cow-Tipping Tag (page 121) inside the goal-kick line of the soccer field, and you might remind players of the safest way to "push" the cows over — that is, that you gently tap them, and the cows do the work of falling over themselves. If you are playing a game that traditionally involves hiding, such as Cops and Robbers (page 128), be clear if some area – the woods – for instance, is out of bounds, and if there is no hiding in your version of the game.

The best way to start a game is to introduce the rules one at a time and allow the participants to practice each rule before you introduce a new one. This can be as simple as everyone practicing moving the imaginary electrical current in Electricity (page 62), or as complex as having everyone practice the elephant position in

Dress Me

PLAYERS 4 or more players. With 10 or more, play as teams and race

EQUIPMENT A large T-shirt, or man's dress shirt for added difficulty

GAME PLAN Move a shirt from one end of a line of kids to the other end of the line.

HOW TO PLAY

Have participants line up side by side. To begin, player one puts on the shirt and holds the hand of the second player.

The shirt must be transferred from the first player to the second player without their breaking hands. It sounds impossible, but it isn't. The other players can help by turning the shirt inside out.

After the shirt is on the second player, the second player holds the hand of a third player, and the transferring continues.

The goal is to move the shirt down the line as quickly as possible.

NOTE Watch out for grabby hands – while this is a great ice-breaker, you shouldn't play it with players who aren't comfortable with a lot of physical contact. Also make sure that the shirt is large enough to fit all of your players.

Speed Rabbit (page 77). By introducing rules gradually, particularly in complicated games, you give players a chance to absorb the rules and practice the skills necessary to succeed or at least keep up.

We usually play two or three practice rounds, especially if we are playing an elimination game. We also sometimes wait to introduce complex rules until after a few practice rounds. For example, in Soh Koh No (page 64), we will have a few rounds of just Soh and

Koh before we complicate things by adding the No.

Always be sure the participants know the rules to the game, and even if everyone groans and says, "Yes, we've played European Handball before," do a quick recap in case someone is too shy to admit otherwise.

Finally, start a game with a clear signal, so that everyone knows the game has started. A good old-fashioned "game on!" does the trick!

Hula Hoop Pass

PLAYERS 6 or more; with 12 or more, play as teams and race

EQUIPMENT One or more large hula hoops

GAME PLAN Move a hula hoop down a line of hand-holding players.

HOW TO PLAY

Have the players line up, holding hands with each other.

Starting with the hula hoop at one end of the line, ask the players to move the hula hoop down the line by stepping through it.

If there is any break in hand-holding, the hula hoop has to start back at the beginning of the line.

Play as a race with teams or just time your group to see how fast they can go.

VARIATIONS

For added difficulty, add multiple or smaller hula hoops.

MODIFICATIONS

For children who will have difficulty moving through the hula hoop on their own, allow a break of hands as long as other parts of the body are touching (for instance, feet, elbows or hips).

Peaking Games

Many of the games in this book do not have set endings. This is because one of the most challenging things about being a leader is knowing when to end, or "peak," a game. Beginning leaders can make the mistake of letting the game drag on until the players are bored and tired. Participants may get crabby and misbehave, spoiling the game or fighting with group members. The next time the leader tries to play that game, the players groan and complain, remembering only the fighting instead of the game itself.

To avoid this, no matter how much fun the group is having, stop the game when all players are excited and engaged. A "last minute of play" is often helpful to players who have difficulty with change, or who are trying to make a last-minute attempt to clinch a championship.

Games that involve elimination may appear to have a natural ending when one player wins the game. However, this does not mean you have to wait until there is a clear "winner" before peaking the game.

Similarly, restrict the number of times you repeat a game that finishes quickly.

It is a good sign if you end the game and the players all whine, "Aww, do we have to stop playing?"

Name Dropping

PLAYERS 10 or more

EQUIPMENT A large sheet (a parachute will also work well)

GAME PLAN Remember everyone's name at the drop of the parachute.

HOW TO PLAY

Divide the group into two teams and have them huddle apart with a space in between.

Stand between the two groups holding up a large sheet or parachute spread out so that neither group can see the other. (It makes it easier if you have two leaders holding the sheet.)

Have each group pick one person to go up to the sheet.

When both players are in place, drop the sheet. The competitors then have to try to say the other person's name first.

Whoever says his opponent's name fastest (and correctly) wins the round and the slower player joins the faster player's team.

Repeat the routine until at least until everyone has had a turn at the sheet. You can continue playing longer, until one team has all of the players, until everyone has learned everyone else's name, or until the game has "peaked."

MODIFICATIONS

Once the players get to know each other better, increase the difficulty level by combining names with favorites such as food, television shows, school subjects or animals.

NOTE For more parachute games, see page 78.

Blind Man's Bluff

PLAYERS 6 or more

EQUIPMENT A long stick (yard or meter stick, baseball bat, etc.)

GAME PLAN Recognize the sound of other players' voices while blindfolded.

HOW TO PLAY

Set up fairly close boundaries for the game. (The playing field should not be the size of an entire field or gym!)

Choose one player to be the Blind Man. He must wear a blindfold and hold a long stick, and wander around the playing field, being guided to stay within the field limits.

The other players mingle, walking around the Blind Man until he taps his stick on the floor three times – and then they all have to stand still.

The Blind Man then holds his stick out, and the player closest to him must silently step forward and hold the other end of the stick. Then the Blind Man asks the other player to say a short word or make an animal noise (like an elephant or a monkey, for example).

The Blind Man will try to guess the name of the player based on his or her voice. If he guesses correctly, the other player becomes the Blind Man.

MODIFICATIONS

More advanced players will try disguising their voices or standing up tall or bending short to fool the Blind Man.

Move Your Butt

PLAYERS Any number

EQUIPMENT None, chairs or hula hoops optional

GAME PLAN Move when something describing you is called; find out what you have in common with other group members.

HOW TO PLAY

Have the group sit or stand in a circle and have It stand in the middle. You will want to start as It the first time you introduce this game.

Explain that It is going to tell them to "move their butts" if whatever It says applies to them. For example, It might say "move your butt if you have a pet," or "move your butt if you had cereal for breakfast," or "move your butt if your favorite food is pizza."

When It calls the command, all players who have a pet (or had cereal or like pizza) must switch spots with someone else who also has a pet (or had cereal or likes pizza).

While players are switching spots, It tries to steal the open spaces. The person who is left in the middle becomes It and must think of something different to get people moving.

VARIATIONS

For a G-rated version without the word "butt," call the game Switch It Up, Change Your Spot, or some similar name, so the command becomes "switch it up if you have a pet."

If the purpose of the game is to learn more about the players, you can call it Have You Ever? and have players switch seats if what is said applies to them. For example, if Vivien says, "Have you ever swum in the ocean?" and Lizzie has swum in the ocean, she must leave her seat and find a new one. Just make sure participants ask age-appropriate questions.

This game can also be played as a parachute game (see Color Exchange, page 81).

MODIFICATIONS

For children who are extra competitive, use hula hoops to designate "spaces" and play the game standing, reducing the potential for injury that happens when competitive children fight over spots in chairs with metal edges.

To increase the difficulty level, do not allow players to say "move your butt if you're wearing blue" or other physical appearance-based orders.

Additionally, you can require It to share the description she uses to order her fellow players. For example, if Tabitha says, "Move your butt if you live in an apartment," she must live in an apartment.

To decrease the difficulty level, the leader of the game can call all the orders.

Play the Game

Our number one recommendation for camp counselors, program leaders, teachers and parents is to play the game along with the participants.

By doing this, you model what active participation and good sportsmanship look like. You are in close proximity to the game and the players, which increases safety and supervision. You can model the skills necessary to play the game. You can make an extra effort to include weaker or less popular players who may not get as many turns or opportunities otherwise.

And if you have fun, your more reluctant participants will see that the game is fun, and will follow your example!

A wee word of warning: when playing with children much smaller than you, be aware of your body and keep your competitive instinct under control, or else you might accidentally body-check little Sally.

Frozen Ts

PLAYERS 4 or more

EQUIPMENT Plastic bag, old T-shirts, water, freezer

GAME PLAN Be the first team to thaw out a T-shirt enough to wear it.

HOW TO PLAY

Split participants up into even groups. (Group size will depend on number of participants and skill level.)

Present each group with a plastic bag. Inside will be an old, large T-shirt that you have frozen in advance.

Teams have to compete to thaw out their T-shirt enough so that one of their team members can wear it.

First team wearing their T-shirt wins. This is literally an ice-breaker!

VARIATIONS

To make the game more challenging and more of a team-builder, play the game so that all team members, rather than just one, must take turns wearing the shirt to be declared the winners.

I Love Marmalade

PLAYERS Any number

EQUIPMENT None

GAME PLAN Move when something you love is described; find out what you have in common with other group members.

HOW TO PLAY

Tell the group that you are going to play a game about things they love, and ask players to think of at least three things that they really love.

Establish square boundaries slightly smaller than the average classroom. Have the entire group stand against one "wall" – for example, the south wall.

The game begins when one player walks to either the east or the west wall, and proclaims his or her love. For example, Rosemary might walk to the east wall and say, "I love marmalade."

All players who love marmalade would join Rosemary on the east wall. Any player who merely likes or is okay with or doesn't like marmalade must go to the west wall. There is no middle ground: you either love the item or you don't.

The next player, Dave, might say, "I love the Beatles," and then walk to either the north wall or the south wall. Those who love the Beatles would join Dave on his wall, and those who do not love the Beatles would line up on the opposite wall. The game proceeds until all the players have declared their love, or until it is peaked.

VARIATIONS
Move Your Butt is a similar game.

NOTE You can either choose which players will proclaim their love in advance or players can choose themselves as the game progresses by taking initiative and beginning to walk. Some leaders like to go in alphabetical order, or by an order established by a previous game. With enthusiastic groups, we prefer to call out the order ourselves to ensure that shy players get a chance to proclaim their love.

Team Jump Rope

PLAYERS Any number

EQUIPMENT A super-long jump rope, or many smaller jump ropes tied together

GAME PLAN Get everyone through the rope without missing a beat.

HOW TO PLAY

This game is best played on a large space with a smooth surface. Two people (either leaders or players not jumping) turn the end of the long rope.

Have players line up and jump through the rope, first one at a time for two beats, then one at a time for one beat, then one at a time with no beats in between. You can vary the number of beats in between players and also vary how long the players stay within the rope.

For better jumpers, increase the number of players jumping at a time. So, for example, the first player jumps in and stays for two turns; the second player jumps in on the first player's second turn and stays for two turns, etc.

This is a task that emphasizes teamwork. Show-boaters or people who do fancy jumps may look cool when they are in the rope, but they are responsible for the next person in line. If one player doesn't get out in time because she is doing a fancy spin, then the next player won't get in!

VARIATIONS

Increase the difficulty level by increasing the number of players jumping: we've seen as many as five people in the rope at the same time!

NOTE As tempting as it may be, do not play Team Jump Rope as an elimination game: it defeats the purpose of building a team of people who support each other, even if one team member can never seem to make it through the rope without getting caught. When we play, we have a rule that the team is not allowed to groan when someone gets caught; they must cheer instead.

Equipment

If your school, camp, recreational program or house has a small budget, and you need to maximize the fun while minimizing cost, we suggest purchasing, begging or borrowing the following items:

- medium-sized utility ball
- tennis ball
- beanbags (6 or more)
- extra-long skipping rope
- Frisbee
- hula hoops (4 or more)

If you have a little more spending power, we suggest upgrading by adding these items:

- parachute
- pylons (4 or more)
- soccer ball
- basketball

If your program really wants to up the fun quotient, we suggest adding:

- hula hoops (class set)
- hockey sticks (class set)
- pool noodles
- football
- funny bounce balls
- scoops (class set)
- extra large utility ball
- baseball bat
- tennis racket

Name Ball Bounce

PLAYERS 8 or more

EQUIPMENT A tennis or utility ball

GAME PLAN Pass the ball around the circle and learn everyone's name.

HOW TO PLAY

Have the group form a circle either sitting or standing. Go around the circle and have everyone say his or her name out loud.

Depending on how many times your group has met each other, you might go around the circle more than once, or play this game after you have played one or two other name games. (See My Name Is Aaron, page 16, Name Dropping, page 19, and Go! at page 24.)

The first player bounces or tosses the ball toward a player across the circle, saying the second player's name as the ball is in the air or bouncing on the ground.

The second player picks a different player to bounce or toss the ball to, and says that player's name.

The game can then go one of two ways. First, you can keep playing and passing the ball around the circle, stopping every 10 or so bounces and asking people who haven't been passed the ball yet to say their names.

Encourage the players to pick different people in the group and emphasize that the point of the game is not to go as quickly as possible, but to ensure all team members are included.

VARIATIONS

The second way you can play this game is by forming a pattern so that the players always pass to the same person. For example, Francis always passes to Jackson, Jackson always passes to Jamal, Jamal always passes to Saifa. If you play this way, the object of the game is to pass the ball around the circle as quickly as possible.

MODIFICATIONS

Increase the difficulty level by adding a requirement that the ball be passed in a certain way. For example, the ball must not hit the ground, the ball must bounce twice, or the ball must be thrown backward through the legs.

If you have players with poor hand-eye coordination, encourage all participants to pass to and receive from someone nearby.

Life Raft

PLAYERS 6 or more

EQUIPMENT A blanket

GAME PLAN Fit everyone onto the life raft, and then make it smaller, and then flip it!

HOW TO PLAY

Tell the group that you have been thrown off a sinking ship onto a life raft. Surrounding you are sharks, and you want to make sure everyone survives.

Squeeze the entire group onto a blanket. Once everyone is on the life raft, change the situation to challenge the players. Ask, "What would happen if the life raft were smaller? Would we still all survive?" Then, fold the blanket so the life raft is half its size, and see if everyone can still fit.

Then unfold the blanket back to its original size and "discover" that there are sealed pockets on the underside of the raft containing food that could help you all survive until the coast guard comes. Tell the group they must work together to flip over the raft without anyone falling off.

This game can be quite challenging, and involves a lot of squeezing together and careful folding of the blanket!

VARIATIONS

You can build up to Life Raft by playing a game of The Shark (page 102) first.

MODIFICATIONS

The size of blanket and number of people will obviously change the difficulty level, so try to make both variables appropriate to your group. A larger raft could be quite challenging for young players.

Go!

PLAYERS At least 8, but 15 or more is the most fun

EQUIPMENT None

GAME PLAN Learn everyone's name and develop teamwork and listening skills.

HOW TO PLAY

Have the group stand in a circle and ask each player to say his or her name out loud.

The game starts when the leader points at a person across the circle and orders that person to Go. For example, if Samantha begins by pointing at Amir and saying, "Go, Amir," Samantha then has to walk toward Amir.

But before Samantha gets to Amir, Amir has to pick someone else across the circle and order him to go. Amir must not leave his spot until he orders someone else.

After Amir has said, "Go, Richard" (for example), he then may leave his spot in the circle, walk toward Richard, and Samantha takes Amir's spot.

Once the ordering has gone around the circle a few times and each person has been picked at least once, you may increase the difficulty by adding a second "Go!" energy so that two orders are taking place at the same time.

VARIATIONS

If you like this game, try playing Ho!

MODIFICATIONS

To increase teamwork and non-verbal communication skills, have players remain silent and just use eye contact to keep everyone engaged in the game.

Ho!

PLAYERS At least 8, but 15 or more is the most fun

EQUIPMENT None

GAME PLAN Pass energy around the circle in a super-fast jumping double high-five.

HOW TO PLAY

Have the group stand in a circle. Ask a player to help you demonstrate what a jumping double high-five looks like: you should jump at the same time and high-five with both hands while they are in the air. Have the first player pick another player and demonstrate what a jumping double high-five looks like, only this time ask the players to shout "Ho!" (or some other monosyllabic word of excitement) as their hands meet in the air.

The game begins when one player runs across the circle to another player and does a jumping double high-five with a "Ho!" in the air. When both players land, they switch places so that the second player is now running across the circle toward another player. And then that player will run across the circle to high-five another player, and so on.

Encourage the other players to stay on their toes and watch for players coming at them. Eye contact is important in this game – if someone approaches you, ready to jump and switch places, you need to be ready or else you might get jumped on!

Also, a jumping double high-five can be a tricky skill to master, and eye contact helps ensure that both players jump at the same time and the same height (which is particularly important when playing with children of different sizes).

Keep going until everyone has been picked at least once.

VARIATIONS

If you need a calmer version of this game, try playing Go!

MODIFICATIONS

Once the game has gone around the circle a few times and each person has been picked at least once, you can increase the difficulty level by adding a second jumping double high-fiver to the bunch. You can even add a third or, depending on the size of your group, a fourth jumper, but a word of warning: the more players you have running at top speed through the middle of the circle, the more chance your players have of bumping into each other.

Modifying Games for Abilities

How would you like to be sitting on the sidelines while all your friends had fun playing games without you because you could not keep up? What if there were ways that you could be included and play as an equal? An inclusive program will allow all participants, regardless of physical, intellectual, developmental and emotional ability, to participate meaningfully, actively, and in a way that challenges them.

We have heard horror stories of children who use mobility devices such as wheelchairs and walkers being relegated to the role of goal-keeper (or even worse, goal posts) because they cannot move around as quickly as the other participants.

This is unacceptable: it teaches the child and the group that the child with special needs is not worth the effort it would take to modify the game.

Does this mean you have to give up soccer and play "everyone wins" games the whole time? No! It does mean that you have to stretch your imagination and find ways to modify the game so that everyone is playing by the same kooky, inclusive rules.

Modifications should rarely, if ever, be made just for the child with special needs. For example, if a child with a visual impairment needs someone to escort her around the bases in soccer baseball, then everyone should run the bases in pairs.

Human Knot

PLAYERS Best with 7 to 15 players

EQUIPMENT None

GAME PLAN Participants form a circle while holding hands.

HOW TO PLAY

This game is not as easy as it first sounds! Have the group stand in a circle and tell everyone to put both hands into the middle of the circle.

Tell the players to grab one person's hand. With their remaining free hand, they should grab a different person's hand. Everyone should be holding hands with two different people.

Then tell them they have to untangle themselves into a circle without breaking hands. This will involve some complicated contortions, going over, under and through the spaces created by the arms. They will have to communicate with each other to figure this out together.

Participants can change the position of their hands to make them more comfortable, but they cannot let go and undo the knot.

This is a great team-builder activity and especially good for leadership training. However, players with less tolerance for physical contact may be uncomfortable, especially if you play it at the beginning of your program.

VARIATIONS

Divide large groups into two or three smaller groups and have them race each other. Not only does this spread the players out to minimize claustrophobia, it also makes for a much faster game.

MODIFICATIONS

Most of the time, the group will end up able to make a circle, but occasionally they will end up with two or three circles. As the leader, you can help them solve the puzzle by encouraging them to make particular moves, or, if the game is going on too long, you can declare Knot First Aid, and allow one or more "knots" to undo and then regrip in a different position.

For players with mobility challenges, using small pieces of rope or cloth to hold on to makes stepping through open spaces much easier.

Inclusion Is for Everyone

- Allow time for breaks or rotations so that students with low energy levels can "tag out" of a game when they need a break.
- Allow extra hits, tries or bounces.
- Change the size of the playing field.
- If any of your participants uses a wheelchair, play soccer on a smooth indoor surface and have everyone use hockey sticks instead of their feet.
- Use balls with holes or with a squishy texture to make them easier to grab.
- Use lighter striking implements (for example, a foam bat with a flat side instead of a baseball bat; a lighter, shorter tennis racket with a larger head).
- Use a football instead of a regular utility ball, which will make it difficult for everyone to catch after it bounces, and not just children with poor hand-eye coordination.
- Use beach balls or balloons, or other larger, lighter and softer balls to slow the pace of the game, increase the time the ball is in the air and reduce the distance the ball can travel.

- Use pinnies so that players can easily identify who is on whose team.
- Pretend you are a football or soccer referee: use your hands, your whistle, your voice, and flags or cards to communicate when the game is stopping and starting, and when rules are broken.
- For tag or capture games, pair slower players with faster players as "running buddies." Both must be tagged before they are captured.
- Use stations to offer a variety of activities. For example, in a relay race, players may choose to either spin around a bat three times, or hula-hoop three times, or count to five three times. Both activities take up approximately the same amount of time, but some may be easier to complete than others.
- Play games that do not require complicated skills and are based more on random chance and raw enthusiasm than on actual ability.

Bending the Rules

It is at times possible to bend the rules without drawing attention to the change. For example, in a game that involves quickly catching and throwing a ball, you might allow a player with special needs to hold on to the ball longer. This type of inclusion does not necessarily need to be announced to the group, nor does everyone have to hold on to the ball for the exact same amount of time.

Children are surprisingly perceptive, and most likely already understand that James is different from them and needs extra help and support. If a player does object or cry foul when you bend the rules, take the player aside and explain that your goal is to help all players succeed at the game. Tell her that you let James hold on to the ball for longer because you want to encourage him to keep playing the game. Depending on the maturity level of the child, you might even consider asking her to look out for and find ways to keep James included in the game: children often find solutions to inclusion that we can't.

Inclusion should always be coordinated with the child's support network, including fellow leaders and teachers, parents, special support staff, and the child herself. Ayeesha may be able to articulate what rule changes help her play the game. Alternatively, Ayeesha's mother or father may be able to talk about her favorite games, and help you identify her strengths, her challenges and her goals.

Inclusion reminds us to focus on the child's strengths as a person rather than the child's challenges. Nicholas who has attention difficulties can quickly become Nicholas with ADD, or even worse: that ADD kid, Nicholas. For example, when we think about that ADD kid, Nicholas, we think about all the games he struggles with because he has ADD. When we think about Nicholas, who just happens to also have attention difficulties, we leave room to think about Nicholas, who is great at Ford Angular Gearbox (page 83) and loves welcoming new people to the group.

String Toss

PLAYERS Groups of 8 to 12

EQUIPMENT A ball of yarn for each group

GAME PLAN Create a web connecting all players.

HOW TO PLAY

Arrange the participants in groups of 8 to 12 players, and have each group sit in a circle.

Give one player in each group a ball of yarn. That person has to find the end of the ball and then toss the ball to anyone else in the circle while still holding on to the end of the yarn. Then the tosser must ask that player one or two questions.

If Walker, for instance, tosses the ball of yarn to Tess, he might ask her, "What is your favorite color?" and "What animal are you most afraid of?" Then Tess has to answer the question and hold on to her part of the yarn and toss the rest of the ball to someone else who hasn't received it yet. If Tess tosses the ball to Marin, she might ask her, "What is your favorite song?" and "What is your least favorite food?"

Play continues until everyone is holding on to a piece of the yarn and you have created a web that includes all the players.

NOTE You won't need a full ball of yarn for this game. For a group of 12, a length of string around 25 yards should do.

Darling, If You Love Me

PLAYERS 8 or more

EQUIPMENT None

GAME PLAN Make the other players smile, and resist when they try to make you smile.

HOW TO PLAY

Have the group sit in a circle with one player in the middle.

If Jackie is the player in the middle, she must go up to the players sitting around the circle one by one and say, "Darling, if you love me, won't you please, please smile?" The idea is to do this in a funny way to make the other players smile.

Any player thus addressed then has to respond, "Darling, you know I love you, but I just can't smile" — without smiling.

If that person can answer without smiling, Jackie moves on to someone else.

If that person does smile, then Jackie gets to join the circle and the player caught smiling has to move to the middle of the circle. The game begins again with a new round.

We encourage as many kooky approaches as possible. We had a friend who would do gymnast stunts as she approached. It was difficult not to smile at someone somersaulting toward you!

MODIFICATIONS

If you find that players are only going to their own friends, or those select few who are just "smiley people," have the player in the middle go around to all the players in the circle in the order they are sitting in.

NOTE Eye contact is mandatory, but touching the other person is off limits. Touching leads to tickling, which can make everybody smile but can also lead to inappropriate touching.

Shoe Pile

PLAYERS Any number

EQUIPMENT None

GAME PLAN Match the shoes to the people.

HOW TO PLAY

This simple game is a good way to have the members of your group meet each other.

Have everyone in your group take off one shoe and throw it into a big pile. Then have each participant pick up a different shoe from the pile and find the person it belongs to.

Players should spend a little time finding out the name of their shoe-match buddies and three things about them that they didn't already know, and then all should gather again in a circle. They will take turns going around the circle introducing their buddies and telling the three things about them to the group.

VARIATIONS

Play multiple rounds of this game, and make it a contest to see who can remember the most about all their partners.

MODIFICATIONS

Have non-verbal participants make up a signature dance move or secret handshake instead of introducing their partner in a more conventional manner.

Many children with attention difficulties also have short-term memory challenges. Help these children to write down key words or draw symbols that will help them remember what they have learned about their partner.

LEADERSHIP ACTIVITIES

We always say the number one rule at camp is to "Have Fun," but often we have loftier ambitions for our participants. The same is true in schools – in gym class, we want to teach them to volley and dribble, but there's more to it than that. Often, our goals when working with children and youth include helping develop their skills at communication, cooperation and leadership. These important life skills are essential for older participants as they head off into the great wide wonder that is the adult world.

We've included some of our favorite activities that inspire the participants to work cooperatively, question their own opinions, listen carefully and value the team effort.

We would definitely include these games in any leader-in-training program.

Be warned: these are not easy activities! After playing the game and discovering the solution, take the time to go through with the players and discover what elements they found challenging, frustrating and exciting. This can often help cement their understanding of skills they learn from what can often slip under the radar as just a "fun game."

Included with each game are Debrief Questions to help get you started. It is important to encourage players to cooperate, listen and self-reflect. Value their opinions and let them make mistakes – don't simply guide them to the right solution!

Cooperative Rocks

PLAYERS Best with 10 or more

EQUIPMENT Two hula hoops, 16 beanbags (or more)

GAME PLAN Get all of the beanbags into your hula hoop.

HOW TO PLAY

Divide the participants into two teams.

Place two hula hoops on the ground, some distance apart, with 16 or more beanbags inside each. Each hula hoop belongs to one of the teams.

Tell participants that "you win when all the beanbags are in your team's hula hoop." Gameplay proceeds with members of each team running to the opposing team's hula hoop and bringing back beanbags one at a time to their own hoop.

The game will go on and on as the participants run beanbags back and forth. However, if the teams are evenly split and there is no cheating, there should be no winner. Make sure each runner takes only one beanbag at a time.

Repeat your instructions, and encourage the group to problem–solve to come up with a solution.

Eventually (we hope) somebody will suggest that if you put the two hula hoops over top of each other and all the beanbags inside, both teams will have won. If they don't suggest it, lead them to that conclusion through hints.

DEBRIEF QUESTIONS Were you satisfied with the outcome? What did you find the most frustrating?

Nuclear Reactor

PLAYERS Best with 10 to 20

EQUIPMENT String, large rubber band, small light objects (for example, shoebox, cup, ping pong ball)

GAME PLAN Work together to move the volatile nuclear objects without touching them.

HOW TO PLAY

The goal of this game is to work cooperatively to "disable" a volatile nuclear reactor. However, since it's radioactively charged, the group can't actually touch any of the parts with their hands, or even get close. Instead, they must use an ordinary, large rubber band.

Set up the game on the floor in an area big enough that players can sit or lie on their stomachs in a circle around the "reactor."

Tie a series of strings to the rubber band, set it down in the middle of the floor and fan the strings out in a circle. Each participant gets a string to hold on to.

Have players stretch, tighten and otherwise manipulate the rubber band by pulling and slacking their strings. Then set them a task – something they have to move.

The "parts" of the "nuclear reactor" that the participants are attempting to move with this contraption are scattered over the center of the circle. They can be everyday objects such as plastic cups, ping pong balls, or anything that isn't too heavy.

You can ask players to do all kinds of things. Have them pick up and drop a ping pong ball into a cup of water. Or give them a series of tasks. For instance, have them turn a box upside down, place a cup upside down on the box, and then carefully place a film canister full of water on top.

DEBRIEF QUESTIONS What worked? What didn't? Were you able to have your ideas heard?

Minesweeper

PLAYERS 6 or more

EQUIPMENT Sidewalk chalk or masking tape

GAME PLAN Have the whole team successfully navigate a minefield.

HOW TO PLAY

Create a grid (for example, 5 feet by 5 feet) using sidewalk chalk or masking tape. Each square of the grid should have enough space for a player to stand inside it fully.

You will have created a sheet of paper with a replica of the grid drawn on it, only with a (fairly) complex path through the grid.

Have the group line up at the starting side. One at a time, they attempt to find the path, but they don't always get far.

For example, the first player, Luke, could step on a wrong square (and thus, a mine), and you would call out, "BOOM," and Luke would be sent back to the beginning of the race. But Drew, the second player, will now know not to begin on that square, and may try another one successfully.

Any time a player steps out of the safe path, you will say, "BOOM" and that player will be sent back to the beginning.

The group will have completed the challenge when every member of the team successfully navigates through the squares. Even if just one player steps out of line, the entire group has to do it all over again.

MODIFICATIONS

If there are players with an intellectual disability that would make it difficult to remember, or if they just have poor memory skills, use a buddy system for everyone to help navigate through the minefield.

Or encourage the group to try going through all together instead of at one time. This will likely prevent frustration or targeting of individuals who some may see as "hindering" the process. Emphasize that you are going through as a team, and everyone must help everyone else navigate the field.

DEBRIEF QUESTIONS What was the hardest part of this activity? Were you able to understand your teammates? What techniques worked for you and your team?

Helium Stick

PLAYERS 6 to 15

EQUIPMENT A very long pole (such as a tent pole, wooden dowel, stick)

GAME PLAN All together now, lower the pole.

HOW TO PLAY

Tell the group that they have a really simple task. Arrange the players in two lines facing each other at arms' length and tell them to each hold out one arm with two fingers extended. Make sure all the fingers are held out at the same level, and then lay the pole so it rests on all the fingertips. Tell players that as a group, they have to lower the stick down to the ground.

Then tell them that there's a further requirement. Every player must keep their fingers making contact with the pole at all times.

Tell the group that it won't be as easy as they think since before they arrived you pumped the stick full of helium so it floats. What really happens is that as they all try to keep their fingers making contact, the stick will naturally begin to rise. There may be lots of arguing and blame assigned.

Eventually they'll figure out that it takes a lot of concentration to work together as a group.

DEBRIEF QUESTIONS What was stopping the helium stick from sinking? What helped you lower the stick? What was the most frustrating part? What was the most satisfying part?

Pass the Ball

PLAYERS 8 or more

EQUIPMENT A small ball

GAME PLAN To pass the ball around as quickly as possible.

HOW TO PLAY

At first, players will laugh and think this game is too easy. But it is really a problem-solving exercise.

Get them to form a circle, and give one of the players a small ball (such as a tennis ball).

Tell him to pass the ball to somebody across the circle. That player must then pass it to somebody else, who will pass it across to someone, and so on. Continue to pass the ball across the circle until everyone has had the ball one time.

Once the ball reaches the final person, ask the group if they remember the order in which they passed the ball. Tell them to do it again, in the same order, but that you'll be timing how fast they can pass the ball around the group in the same sequence.

Let them do this a few times, but then tell them the ball can be passed to all the players much faster than that.

Inevitably, eventually, one person will ask if the group can rearrange themselves so that they are standing in a circle in the order they pass the ball. Of course, this isn't against the rules, so let them go ahead. This will shave off some time.

After a few more rounds somebody will ask if the ball has to be thrown or just touched by every member. Again, this isn't against the rules.

Encourage the group to try different ways of getting it around the circle in a few seconds. A few rounds later, announce that it can be done in under a second. See how long it takes for the group to figure out a solution.

If all the participants put their hands together to form a ramp and then roll the ball down the hand ramp so that the ball touches every hand in the correct order, it can in fact be done in under a second.

DEBRIEF QUESTIONS What helped make your attempt successful? Did you have any "Ah-ha!" moments? Any moments where you wanted to give up?

The Elephant Game

PLAYERS At least 5

EQUIPMENT None required

GAME PLAN Copy or guess the actions.

HOW TO PLAY

Have players sit in a circle or audience formation. Pick three players to move away from the group, so they can't see or hear what is happening. Be the leader or choose an "in-the-know" participant to explain the game to the group.

The players get called back one at a time. When the first player returns, tell her to watch the performance carefully, as she will have to recreate it for the second player.

The leader pretends to wash an elephant: he walks it in, ties it to an imaginary post, picks up a bucket of water, turns on a tap, fills the bucket and walks back to the elephant. He starts by washing the trunk, then behind the ears, then up and down a leg. He splashes water over the side of the body, washes the flank and moves to the next leg. He washes the tail, and then moves to the other side of the elephant, doing the whole thing in reverse. He ends by untying the elephant from the post and walking it "off stage."

The second player is called back in and must watch the first player attempt to copy the performance of the leader. Then the third player is called in and the second player must attempt to copy the performance. Finally, the third player gives his version of the performance, and must provide a "play-by-play" description of his actions.

We've seen and heard every possible interpretation, from washing windows to putting up a tent!

DEBRIEF QUESTIONS What did you find difficult or easy about this activity? If you were watching, how did you react when you saw the participants getting confused? If you were acting, how did it feel being asked to imitate something you didn't understand?

NOTE Do not call this the Elephant Game in front of your participants: it will give away the secret!

Leaky Pipes

PLAYERS 8 to 12, divided into 2 teams

EQUIPMENT Hollow pipes with holes, each taped at one end. Access to water or one large bucket filled with water, and smaller buckets.

GAME PLAN Get the ping pong ball out of a pipe without tipping the pipe over.

HOW TO PLAY

Set up this challenge ahead of time. Prepare two PVC pipes each about 4 inches in diameter and at least waist-high; drill a number of small holes all over the side of the pipes and then tape one end closed with duct tape or other heavy duty tape.

Split the group into two teams so that each team has a pipe. Get them to stand the pipes up on end, and then drop a ping pong ball down each and tell them the first team to get their ping pong ball out without tipping the pipe over will win.

The trick that each team should eventually figure out (you will leave the buckets and source of water nearby as a hint) is that they have to fill the pipe with water so the ping pong ball floats to the top. Since the pipe is full of holes the whole team has to get involved to help plug the holes using their fingers.

Because the buckets you set out will be small, there will be a lot of running back and forth to fetch the water. Players will get wet, of course.

DEBRIEF QUESTIONS Would you have been able to do this on your own? How can you translate the lesson learned here to problems in real life?

Tips on Training Leaders

Whether you are a supervisor starting out a camp program, a counselor coaching a leader-in-training, a teacher working with a teacher candidate, or a parent trying to show your eldest child how to baby-sit your youngest child, you must not only teach your protégé the ins and outs of policy, procedure and safety, you must also teach them how to play with kids.

Playing the game with the kids in your program is the best way to role-model enthusiasm and participation, and to monitor their behavior (see page 20, Play the Game for more about that). Playing with your leaders is also the best way to develop their skills as leaders.

When we were first-year camp counselors, the only games we knew were games that we ourselves had played in childhood. And yet, in less than a week, were expected to go from ordinary citizens to game-playing hyper-energized camp counselors extraordinaire. Fortunately, out of our four training days, our mentors spent a full day playing games with us, and also included game play throughout the more policy-driven sections of our training. This time was invaluable, as we not only added a variety of games to our toolkit, we also learned:

- To explain rules through step-by-step demonstration,
- To use funny accents, personas or themes to make the games special,
- To boast about our own undefeated record at a game, so as to inspire our players to defeat us,
- To spin tales of epic proportions about the origins of the game, whether it be the mystical ancient forces in Soh Koh No (page 64) or the location of a dragon's secret power in Dragon Tails (page 115).

This "play the game" attitude can be carried forward to all aspects of your training sessions. Want to teach them how to run a theme day? Run a theme day yourself, and have your leaders go through the events as if they were campers. Want to teach them how to deal with a lost child? Hide a beanbag or a fellow staff member and have them simulate the lost child procedure. Want to show them how to deal with rule breakers? Assign each leader a stereotypical childhood behavior and role-play various behavior management scenarios.

Evaluating Leaders

Evaluating your leaders and leaders-in-training is an essential part of their development: without constructive criticism, they will not know how to improve. Your program may require you to evaluate your staff in a formal written document that could be placed in their employee records and used to determine staff promotions as well as future job recommendations. However, we aren't going to address the nitty gritty of that type of evaluation here, as those will most likely be determined by the type of program you are running. Instead, we'd like to offer some quick tips on how to evaluate leaders on an ongoing basis:

- Stop by their groups to play with them often. If you are a leader supervising a leader-in-training, play the game with them as a participant rather than watching with a checklist from the sidelines. Talk to your LITs afterward and give them specific suggestions or praise.
- Catch them being good. Thank them for special efforts they have made, either in programming or in connecting with their participants.
- Make specific comments such as "I really loved that new game you were just playing," or "Next time you're walking past a muddy stream, you should tell your campers not to get their feet wet before they are close enough to jump in."
- Ask specific questions to get them to reflect on their own abilities and progress, such as "I saw you struggling to get Byron to participate. What strategies did you try to get him on board?"
- If you notice a learning leader having a hard time with a particular camper, sit down and come up with a list of strategies that he or she can try.
- Encourage them to lead the problem-solving effort by disciplining the camper themselves, where possible. Stepping in as the all-powerful supervisor robs them of their own authority.

We find that it is always better to provide specific verbal feedback in advance of more formal written feedback. This allows the leader time to improve his or her skills almost instantly.

Above all else, remember that your leaders or leaders-in-training are people too, and enjoy a pat on the back or a high five just as much as the youngest children in your program.

Take It Easy

ONCE YOUR KIDS HAVE SETTLED IN and got to know you and each other, you can begin the real fun. The games in this chapter might require less physical energy, but they are by no means "easy" games. Many of them require thinking, strategizing or problem solving. Some of them are based on luck and require no specific skills. Some of them are quieter games, but many of them can get quite exciting and noisy.

On the whole, these games require little to no physical movement and are perfect for when your children need lower-energy games that aren't lower-fun games. We recommend playing these games on hot days when the sun is highest, and at the beginning and end of the day when participants are just waking up or ready to go to bed.

These games are also great right after a vigorous and exhausting racing game, or immediately after lunch when the sugar high hasn't quite kicked in yet and since running on a full stomach is a bad idea.

Buzz

PLAYERS 2 or more

EQUIPMENT None

GAME PLAN Count to 100 and remember to say "buzz" for 7 or multiples of 7.

HOW TO PLAY

Have your group sit in a circle or rows. Players count off in turn to 100, each saying one number aloud.

The trick is, they must replace the number 7 and all multiples of 7 (14, 21, 28, etc.), including any number with a 7 in it (27, 37) with the word "buzz." The number 77 will be "buzz buzz"!

You can play just for fun and not for competition. Or you can assess penalty points for players who miss a "buzz" or hesitate too long, and the player with the fewest points by you time you reach 100 is the winner.

If the game is moving really slowly or you have a large group, eliminate players after two mistakes, and play until there is only one player left.

VARIATIONS

To make the game easier, try Fizz. Substitute "fizz" for 5 and multiples of 5, since it is easier for most kids to count by 5.

To make the game more difficult, try Fizz Buzz. Substitute "fizz" for 5 and multiples of 5, as well as "buzz" for 7 and multiples of 7! Play begins: "1, 2, 3, 4, fizz, 6, buzz, 8, 9, fizz fizz, 11, 12, 13, buzz, fizz fizz, 16, buzz, 18, 19, fizz...." The number 57 will be "fizz buzz" and 75 will be "buzz fizz"!

MODIFICATIONS

For kids who don't know their times tables at all, change the game so that they say "buzz" every time they have to say 7 (7, 17, 27), or every time they reach a multiple of 10 (10, 20, 30, etc.).

Black Magic

PLAYERS Any number, with 2 leaders

EQUIPMENT None

GAME PLAN Boggle the minds of the players.

HOW TO PLAY

Have the second leader leave the group and go into another room or behind a tree.

Tell the group that the second leader has psychic powers and can guess whatever item the group chooses. Then have the group pick an item, "I Spy" style – for example, a player's blue lunchbox.

Have the second leader come back to the group. Lead the psychic leader through a variety of items – for example, "Did we pick the soccer ball?"

Before you name the item that you and the group chose, ask about an item of the color that you and the second leader agreed upon beforehand. For example, if you agreed on black, "Did we pick the black crayon?"

The item that immediately follows the item of the agreed color will be the chosen item. Magically, the second leader will guess right!

VARIATIONS

When the second leader returns, you can instead start your question with the same letter that the name of the object starts with. For example, say, "What object do you think it is?" if the object is a watch, or "Bet you can't guess what the object is," if the object is a ball.

Charades

PLAYERS Any number

EQUIPMENT Small pieces of paper and a pencil; stopwatch or timer optional

GAME PLAN Guess what object, phrase or title your teammate is acting out.

HOW TO PLAY

Divide the group into two or more teams. Hand each group a set of slips of paper (10 or more).

Have teams quietly come up with target phrases within a given category, for example, books, movies, songs, famous people or popular sayings. Teams should write their chosen target phrases on the slips of paper and then hand them to the leader.

Remember to keep the piles of paper separate: nothing is easier than guessing your own answer.

Choose a team to go first, and a player from that team to draw a slip of paper from the opposite team's pile and act out the charade. Check to make sure the "acting" player understands the clue before you start the timer.

Choose an appropriate amount of time for your age group and skill level: anywhere from 30 seconds for the pros to two minutes for the beginners. Longer than three minutes, and the guessing team will get frustrated and the other team will get bored.

Only the actor's teammates may guess when he is acting: the other team must remain quiet. If the waiting team whispers or accidentally blurts out something, the other team can take advantage of the slip-up and use anything said to help figure out their answer.

The actor attempts to mime (no sound allowed and no mouthing words) the target phrase using a series of charade "conventions." For example:

- Number of fingers held in the air means number of words.

- Number of fingers tapped on the arm means number of syllables.

- Hands on hips means famous person.

- Opening a book or turning pages means book title.

- An old-fashioned camera motion means movie title.

- Opera singer-style posing means song title.

- Tugging on the ear means "sounds like." For example, to act out "rug," tug on your ear and hug yourself.

- A crossing-guard style "stop" motion means "stop with that word, let's move on to the next."

- Making a pinching motion means either a small word or "shorten the word you just said."

- Making a stretching motion as if pulling a rubber band means either a long word or "lengthen the word you just said."

- Shaking your head no means "you're on the wrong track."

- Moving your hands in a circular motion and nodding means "keep going, you're close to the answer."

- Tapping your nose and pointing at the correct guesser means "correct."

If playing in teams, you can compete for the shortest total time required to hit the targets or the greatest number of correct solutions.

VARIATIONS

Similar games include Junior Charades and Pictionary. For a more active version, try Lemonade (page 94).

MODIFICATIONS

For smaller groups, play for individual points rather than group points.

To increase the difficulty level, play individually and have each actor think up his or her own charade on the spot. Alternatively, play with longer clichéd phrases. For an English class, trying quoting Shakespeare!

To decrease the difficulty level, choose easy-to-visualize words or phrases, or come up with all of the phrases yourself. Restrict the category so they are all the same thing. For kids who can't read, whisper the target to them.

Junior Charades

PLAYERS Any number

EQUIPMENT Small pieces of paper and a pencil; stopwatch or timer optional

GAME PLAN Guess what activity or item your teammate is acting out or miming.

HOW TO PLAY

This game might more appropriately be called "guess the mime," as it focuses on identifying activities or objects rather than decoding titles or phrases.

If you have 12 or more players, divide the group into two or more teams. Fewer than 12 players can play in team format or in individual format.

Choose which team will go first, and choose a member from that team to act out the charade. Whisper an activity or object in that player's ear. Some examples include a cell phone, a tree, a book, a pencil, a candle, sweeping, eating carrots, bunny rabbit, riding a bicycle, skiing down a hill, brushing your teeth, washing the dishes or cutting up a loaf of bread.

Check to make sure the "acting" player understands the clue before starting the timer. Like Charades, choose an appropriate amount of time for your age group and skill level: anywhere from between 30 seconds for the pros and two minutes for the beginners. If you go for longer than three minutes, the guessing team will get frustrated and the other team will get bored.

The actor attempts to mime (no sound allowed and no mouthing words) the target activity using a combination of charade conventions and make-believe. For example:

- Pretending to hold something means you are acting out an object (for example, a carrot).
- Swinging your arms like a runner means you are acting out an activity (for example, eating carrots).

- Tugging on the ear means "sounds like." For example, if you wanted to act out "cry" you might tug on your ear and point at your eye.
- Making a pinching motion means either a small word or "shorten the word you just said."
- Making a stretching motion like you were pulling a rubber band means either a long word or "lengthen the word you just said."
- Shaking your head no means "you're on the wrong track."
- Moving your hands in a circular motion and nodding means "keep going, you're close to the answer."
- Tapping your nose and pointing at the correct guesser means "correct."

If playing in teams, you can compete for the shortest total time required to hit the targets or the most number of correct solutions.

VARIATIONS

Similar games are Pictionary and Charades. For a more active version, try Lemonade (page 94).

MODIFICATIONS

For smaller groups, play for individual points rather than group points. For example, if you guess the charade, you get two points, and if you successfully act out your charade, you get one point, or vice versa.

For younger players, allow them to make some noise as long as they do not refer to the clue directly. For example, if the target is eating carrots, you might allow them to make munching noises.

For very young players, try Animal Charades, where you restrict the categories to types of animals. In Animal Charades, the players are allowed to make the sound of the animal they are acting out.

Pictionary

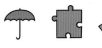

PLAYERS Any number

EQUIPMENT Paper and pencils, or chalk and a chalkboard; stopwatch or timer optional

GAME PLAN To guess what object, person, phrase or title your teammate is drawing.

HOW TO PLAY

Divide group into two or more teams. Hand each group a set of slips of paper (10 or more).

Have both groups quietly come up with target phrases within a given category, for example, books, movies, songs, famous people, or popular sayings. The groups should write their chosen target phrases on the slips of paper and then hand them to the leader. Remember to keep the piles of paper separate.

Choose a team to go first and choose one player from the team to be the first "artist." Pick a target phrase from the opposing team's suggestion pile and hand it to the artist.

Once the artist understands the clue, she can start drawing and you can start the timer. The artist draws on a piece of paper large enough for her team to see.

She is not allowed to mime, make noise, or use letters or numbers in her drawing. She cannot use charade conventions that spell out the category or number of words or syllables; however, she can use charade conventions such as "keep going," "stop and try again," and "on the nose."

Pick an appropriate time-limit for the artist: we suggest anywhere between 30 seconds and three minutes. More than three minutes can be frustrating for the waiting team and for the unsuccessful artist.

Once the team has either successfully guessed the target phrase, or has run out of time, it is the other team's turn. You can play for the lowest cumulative time necessary to solve the clues, or you can play for the most clues guessed.

VARIATIONS

Similar games include Charades and Junior Charades.

MODIFICATIONS

For smaller groups, play for individual points rather than group points. For example, if you guess the picture you get two points, and if you successfully draw your picture, you get one point, or vice versa.

To decrease the difficulty level, choose easy-to-draw words or phrases, or come up with all of the phrases yourself. For players who can't read, whisper the phrase to them.

Creating a Daily Program

1. Planning and changing

The most important part of creating a daily program is understanding that it will change. Whether it changes because of poor weather or poor behavior is irrelevant: emergencies, annoyances or exciting opportunities will arise and your whole program will go out the window. However, it is always better to over-plan: planning actually provides you with many options.

In a day-camp environment, we recommend planning two to three games for every half-hour. Sports, crafts and other activities may take anywhere from half an hour to a full hour. However, games tend to have a shorter lifespan, particularly if you are "peaking" them when you should be (for more on peaking, see page 18).

Most games last 15 to 20 minutes, including about five minutes of introducing the rules of the game, and including enough rounds for everyone to get the hang of the game before elimination begins. However, some exhausting games such as Cow-Tipping Tag (page 121) can last only five minutes or less before everyone is exhausted and falling over.

Planning two games assumes that both of your games will succeed. However, sometimes one of your games may flop. You may have misjudged the energy level, age appropriateness, or ability of your group to play the game. Your group may be getting overly competitive, and that game of Larry, Curly, Moe (page 96) you had planned may turn into Wrestlemania. We recommend either planning three games for every half-hour, or having a backup list of games that you can turn to if something goes wrong.

2. Energy watch

The second most important part of creating a daily program is getting to know the energy level of your players during the day. For example, many children are resolutely sluggish when their parents drop them off at a full-day program in the morning, and take about a half-hour of "get them moving" games before they can be "run ragged." On the other hand, although children may be on a sugar high after lunch, an exhausting game of tag on a hot day and with a full stomach can lead quickly to upset tummies or worse.

As a general rule, children are most tired at the beginning and end of the day, and just before lunchtime.

These are the times when you want to program quiet, "take it easy" games or activities that require more fine detail work, but are easy to succeed at. If Chris has attention difficulties, an easy craft or card game will keep him focused and keep him sitting quietly.

Remember that bored children and tired children become cranky children: don't exhaust your campers, or give them activities that require too much concentration and skill at the end of the day.

3. Variety

Finally, remember to include a variety of activities. You may love running games and think that they are brilliant for exhausting your players until they are so tired they don't have the energy to misbehave. However, the slower players in your group will get frustrated and disengage if you are playing games that they can never win.

Balance your competitive games and cooperative games, the sports and the activities, the quiet, "get them moving," and "run them ragged" games. Plan special events or mini-competitions at the end of the week, or throw in some theme days (see page 106) to add variety and excitement.

Every day, you should have at least one game that each child in your group can succeed at. This does not mean they have to "win," but they should feel proud of their performance. For example, if you have a child with poor hand-eye coordination, weak fine motor skills and low mobility who has an incredibly expressive face, consider adding a make-believe or drama game to your daily program. Non-athletes may love crafts, brain games or trivia, and athletes may discover they love them too.

Variety is the foundation of an inclusive program: once you create a daily program where each child can succeed at least once, you are closer to your goal of having all children succeed as much as possible.

Sample Programs

Following are two sample programs to demonstrate the importance of variety and planning in a daily program.

Although we've worked with all ages and group numbers, Mary tends to work with older kids (ages 10 to 13) in large groups of 15 or more, and Laura more often works with younger kids (ages 4 to 7) in smaller groups of fewer than 10 players.

For a sample program for a birthday party for a seven-year-old, see page 90.

Mary's big group of older kids

9:00	My Name Is Aaron; Name Dropping
9:30	Cat and Mouse (parachute); Kitty Wants a Corner; Chocolate Factory
10:00	Speedball (backups include European Handball)
10:30	Snack and water, Black Magic
11:00	Kooky Relay; Atom
11:30	Pass the Slap; Up Jenkins; Darling, If You Love Me
12:00	Lunch time!
12:30	Charades; Crambo; Twenty Questions
1:00	The Animal Game; Dragon's Tails; Blob Tag
1:30	Soh Koh No; Predator Prey; Ho!
2:00	Cow-Tipping Tag; Sword in the Stone: Supreme Master of the Universe
2:30	Snack and water; Fizz Buzz
3:00	Bop and Speed Rabbit; Larry, Curly, Moe
3:30	Total Recall; Murder Wink; Evolution
4:00	Kids go home!

Laura's smaller group of younger kids

9:00	Name Ball Bounce; Move Your Butt
9:30	Going on a Picnic; Beans
10:00	Ship to Shore (with Here, There, Where); What Time Is It, Mr. Wolf?
10:30	Snack and water; I Spy
11:00	Silent Ball; Junior Charades
11:30	Chute Ball, Color Exchange, Cat and Mouse (all with small parachute)
12:00	Lunch time!
12:30	Heads Up, Seven Up; Crambo; Murder Wink,
1:00	Mother, May I?; Spud; Cow-Tipping Tag
1:30	Drip, Drip, Drop; Firefighter Relay
2:00	Dodgeball; Red Light, Green Light; Blob Tag
2:30	Snack and water; Two Truths and a Lie
3:00	Fruit Salad; Steal the Bacon
3:30	CN Tower; Musical Chairs; Dance Freeze
4:00	Kids go home!

Going on a Picnic

PLAYERS Any number

EQUIPMENT None

GAME PLAN Solve the pattern and join the trip.

HOW TO PLAY

Gather your players together. Think up a word pattern but do not tell anyone what it is. For example: hula hoops, giraffes and balloons all fit a double-letter word pattern.

You should then say, "I'm going on a picnic, and I'm bringing..." and suggest a word that fits your pattern. The players take turns saying, "I'm going on a picnic, and I'm bringing..." and suggest a word.

If the word fits your word pattern (for instance, "books," "a ladder," "spaghetti," and "strawberries" all work), you will let them take the item on the picnic, saying "Yes, you can bring strawberries on our picnic."

If it doesn't fit (as, for example, "table," "lemons" and "watermelon" do not fit the above double-letter word pattern), you will say "No, you can't bring a watermelon on our picnic."

The game ends when most or all of the players are able to correctly name items to bring and identify the word pattern.

VARIATIONS

Adapt the adventure according your theme. For example, if you are having a Safari Day, say "I'm going on a safari, and I'm bringing...." Or for a Swim Day, say "I'm going to the pool, and I'm bringing...."

MODIFICATIONS

The pattern can be changed to make it simpler or more complex, depending on the age group. A simple pattern would be words that start with the same letter (apple, ants, an axe) or words describing the same kind of object (apple, peach, banana).

A more difficult pattern could be one in which words have to be in alphabetical order (apple, banana, cactus, dog...).

This Is a What?

PLAYERS Any number

EQUIPMENT A few objects that can be handed around the circle (for instance, a shoe, beanbag, hat, water bottle)

GAME PLAN Pass items around a circle without losing track.

HOW TO PLAY

Have the group sit in a circle. Begin by holding out an object (such as a shoe) to the player sitting next to you, (in this case) Gerard.

Say to Gerard, "This is a shoe."

Gerard has to respond, "A what?"

Say it again: "A shoe."

He says (again), "A what?"

You repeat, "A shoe."

Then Gerard takes the shoe and looks at it and says, "Oh, a shoe."

Gerard then turns to the next person in the circle and restarts the whole routine with her; she, in turn goes on to the person next to her, and so on.

Any time after Gerard has the shoe, you can start a new object, but going in the opposite direction. Confusion will ensue when the two items meet!

Play until the game is peaked.

MODIFICATIONS

To make the game more challenging, you can add more items to pass along, in the same direction as the first, until there are as many objects going around the circle as there are people and everyone is playing at the same time. Pandemonium!

Smog Days

Some parents find themselves reluctant to let their kids play outside when the air quality is poor. Smog and air pollution are major concerns for urban recreational and camp programs that operate primarily outside. While many day camps are based out of community centers — perhaps even with air conditioning — other programs still operate in the good old-fashioned outdoors. Outdoor programs may not have a lot of tree cover or shaded areas to play in. However, just because it is a "smog day," doesn't mean you should stay inside all day! You can and should still try to go outside on smog days, and you can do so safely if you keep the following guidelines in mind.

On smog days, the air is harder to breathe and our bodies get tired faster. Smog days are often accompanied by extreme heat, doubling the danger level for everyone. Smog days are particularly difficult for people with asthma or other respiratory conditions.

Ways to prevent health risks on smog days include:

- Play running games before 10:30 and after 2:30 when the sun isn't as hot. On a day that you know is going to be a smog day, it is often a good idea to play an intense running game first thing in the morning so that your players get some energy released at the safest time of the day.
- Any games that do involve running should be of a shorter duration. For example, play tag for five minutes instead of 10, or play slow-motion or frozen tag (pages 120–121) instead of conventional tag.
- Program more crafts, brain games and quiet games.
- Play water games, or incorporate water into your other games. For example, in some ball-tossing games, you can replace the ball with a wet sponge or turn Hot Potato into Wet Potato (page 148).
- Take frequent food and water breaks. Avoid caffeine or pop: drink fruit juices and water instead.
- Spend time in the shade. If your site doesn't have shade, purchase an inexpensive beach umbrella for the group to sit under during quiet activities.
- Monitor the children's breathing and general level of energy, and modify the program accordingly.
- Make sure everyone wears a hat.
- Encourage participants to wear light-colored, loose-fitting clothing.

Twenty Questions

PLAYERS Any number

EQUIPMENT None

GAME PLAN Guess the hidden target through a series of yes or no questions.

HOW TO PLAY

Ask each player in the group to think of an object.

Most games of Twenty Questions confine the target objects to Animal (may include people), Vegetable or Mineral, but you can open up the categories once you are confident in your group's ability to guess the target objects.

Choose one person to be the first to answer. If Mary is the first answerer, the other members of the group must ask Mary questions that can be answered with a "yes" or a "no" in an effort to narrow down her target object.

For example, one series might be:

- "Is it a vegetable?" No.
- "Is it an animal?" Yes.
- "Is it an animal found in the forest?" No.
- "Is it an animal found in the zoo?" Yes.
- "Is it an animal found in the desert?" Yes.
- "Is it a lizard?" No.
- "Is it a mammal?" Yes.
- "Can it carry people?" Yes.
- "Is it a camel?" Yes!

The person who guesses the target object correctly gets to be the next answerer. If you find one person is regularly guessing the correct answer, you might ask them to choose someone else to be the answerer.

If the target object cannot be guessed by the group within 20 questions, they are "stumped" and the answerer gets another turn.

VARIATIONS

Play Celebrity Twenty Questions: Restrict all of the objects to famous fictional characters or real-life celebrities.

You can also divide your group into teams and play for points.

MODIFICATIONS

To increase the difficulty, remove the restrictions of Animal, Vegetable and Mineral.

To decrease the difficulty level, limit all target objects to one category. For instance, have players choose only animals. You might also want to get the answerer to whisper their object to you, so you can help them answer questions accurately.

Transition Games

We've always found that players enjoy themselves the most when they are actively involved. But often, when we need to get from one place to the other, active engagement falls by the wayside and participants of a camp or school program are simply expected to fall in line and make their way from one spot to the other without any fun to focus their attention. In our experience, this is the sort of situation that breeds fights and behavior problems. In this book, we've included some games and activities that work great while on the move from one spot to the other.

Many of the Brain Game activities, marked with this symbol , are great to keep the fun going while transitioning from one area or activity to another. These games keep participants actively engaged, but don't rely on specific movements or the kind of player set-up that make other games impossible to take on the move.

Going on a Picnic (page 44), Twenty Questions, Two Truths and a Lie (page 47) and I Spy (page 48) are all games easily played on the move, whether you're walking from one location to another, travelling in a car, or taking a long bus ride back from a daytrip.

There are also some active games that involve forward movement that can be modified to help get

Two Truths and a Lie

PLAYERS Any number

EQUIPMENT None

GAME PLAN To try to figure out which statements are truth and which statement is a lie.

HOW TO PLAY

One player thinks up three statements, two of which are true, one that is a lie.

For example, Tom could say "I know how to sail" (truth), "I've ridden in a police car" (truth) and "I love cats" (lie).

The other players must think about what they know about Tom, and figure out which statements are true, and which one Tom is making up. You can run through each statement, asking the other participants, "Who thinks Tom doesn't know how to sail?" and "Who thinks Tom hasn't ridden in a police car?" and so on.

After all participants have made their guesses, Tom reveals which two statements are true and which is false.

NOTE Make sure players have their two truths and lie thought up before their turn, otherwise you'll end up with a lot of "ummm...." as players try to think up creative statements.

players walking (or running) from one area to another.

Playing a modified version of Red Light, Green Light (page 116) can help keep any group focused while on the move. Just call out "Green Light" when you want participants to be moving quickly, "Yellow Light" when you want some slow-motion walking, and "Red Light" if you want participants to stop.

If you see any players moving on "Red Light," send them to the back of the line.

"Mother, May I?" (page 90) can also work in a similar way. "Chuck the Chicken" and its variation, "Kick the Chicken" (page 116), can be great on-the-move games, as long as you insist on the "Chicken" being chucked or kicked in the general direction you want the group to go.

I Spy

PLAYERS Any number

EQUIPMENT None

GAME PLAN Guess the item another player has "found."

HOW TO PLAY

One player is the "Spy." Begin the game as the Spy yourself or choose a player from the group to be the Spy.

The Spy must search around the area for an item, any item, to choose. It should be an item that all members of the group will be able to see. Avoid moving objects, since they may be gone shortly after the Spy has spied them.

The Spy will then say "I spy with my little eye something that is..." and name the color of the object. For instance, when thinking of a blue backpack, "I spy with my little eye something that is blue."

The other players must take turns guessing what the object is. "Is it that car?" "It it William's eyes?" "Is it my towel?" And so on.

The player who guesses the object correctly then becomes the Spy.

VARIATIONS

You could use this game to help enforce understanding of shapes or geometric attributes. For example, "I spy...something that is a circle" or "I spy... something with a right angle."

MODIFICATIONS

For younger players, it is often best to have them tell you, the leader, what item they have decided on. In one Junior Kindergarten classroom, one youngster rejected the guesses of his classmates, and when everyone finally gave up, he had completely forgotten the object that he had selected!

What Has Changed?

PLAYERS Any number

EQUIPMENT None

GAME PLAN Figure out what about a player has changed.

HOW TO PLAY

Pick one player, for example, Ethan, to leave the group first. Have the whole group look carefully at Ethan.

Have Ethan leave the group, either by going just outside of a room or tent, or by hiding behind a tree. When Ethan is away from the group, have him change one or two things about his physical appearance. For example, have him untie his shoelaces, roll up his socks, part his hair differently, or put his hat on backwards instead of forward.

When Ethan returns to the group, players must guess what has changed. The player to guess correctly gets to leave the group and change next.

VARIATIONS

Play with two or three participants leaving the group. They can then change clothes, which can increase the difficulty level. Ensure that if participants are changing in front of each other, they are sticking to items such as socks and jackets, and not trading underwear!

MODIFICATIONS

For younger children, go with them as they "change" so you can ensure that they will actually change something, and so that you know specifically what they have changed.

Total Recall

PLAYERS Any number

EQUIPMENT A variety of different items, a plate, something to cover it all up, pencils and sheets of paper

GAME PLAN Try to remember as many items as possible.

HOW TO PLAY

Tell the players that you will be testing their memory skills. Have a tray or piece of sturdy paper with a variety of items placed on it (for example, a watch, hair elastic, small notebook, whistle, plastic frog, etc.), and a sheet covering the items.

Remove the sheet and tell participants to look carefully at all the items and try to remember as many of the items as possible – without writing any of them down.

After about 20 seconds (time depending on the age of the participants), cover up the items or take them out of view. Then have players, working independently, each make a list of items they remember.

The player who remembers the most items wins the game.

MODIFICATIONS

For younger campers, have fewer items, and consider having them work in pairs or small groups to create a list of items they remember.

You can be the transcriber for teams or individuals who cannot write – just have them whisper their answers to you and write them down yourself.

Rigamarole

PLAYERS Any number, but smaller is better

EQUIPMENT None

GAME PLAN Remember a combination of tongue twisters while counting.

HOW TO PLAY

Have the players sit in a circle and pick a player to start.

The first player is "one" and must choose a phrase of three words – a number, an adjective or descriptor, and a noun – to string together, all based on the "o" sound of "one" – "one oily owl," for example.

The second player must repeat the first phrase, followed by a second phrase based on the "t" sound that starts the number two. For example, "One oily owl, two twisted tortoises."

The third player follows with, "One oily owl, two twisted tortoises, three thumping thunderclaps."

The string of phrases goes around the circle until you reach the number 10, until the group can't remember all the numbers, or until the game is peaked.

MODIFICATIONS

To decrease the difficulty, allow players to pick only a noun instead of a noun and an adjective. Or forget about having them try to remember the preceding phrases, and have them say only their own.

To increase the difficulty, restrict the nouns to animal, vegetable, person or other category, or have players come up with a number of words equal to their starting number – "seven sapphire slippery slimy sneaky scaly snakes," for example.

Pass the Slap

PLAYERS 10 or more

EQUIPMENT None

GAME PLAN Pass a slap around a circle without missing a beat.

HOW TO PLAY

Have the players lie on their stomachs in a circle with their hands out in front of them.

Have the players overlap their hands, so that the hands of their neighbors are in between their own hands. (If the players are Marisa, Robert and Kevin, the hands would be: Robert's left hand, Marisa's right hand, Kevin's left hand, Robert's right hand.)

First practice passing the slap clockwise (to the left). You – or a chosen leader – slap the ground with your left hand, and the hand next to your hand clockwise slaps the ground (note that this is not the next person clockwise!). And then the next hand clockwise slaps the ground, and so on. The slap continues clockwise around the circle.

Next, practice going counterclockwise. The leader slaps the ground, and the hand counterclockwise to (to the right of) the leader's starting hand slaps the ground. The slap continues counterclockwise around the circle.

After you have practiced going around the circle a few times, introduce the double slap. A double slap changes the direction the slap travels.

For example, if a slap comes from Robert's left hand to Marisa's right hand, and Marisa slaps the ground twice, the slap reverses back toward Robert's left hand. If a player misses her turn to slap, or slaps out of turn, she is out.

If this seems confusing, consult the illustration! Once you've practiced a few rounds, this is a fun game to play.

MODIFICATIONS

Can be played around a small table or without elimination.

Crambo

PLAYERS 4 or more

EQUIPMENT None

GAME PLAN Guess the target word through a series of rhyming questions and answers.

HOW TO PLAY

Choose one player – for example, Amrit – to choose a word for the other players to guess.

Amrit might decide that "rug" is his target word, but he must choose other words that rhyme with "rug" to play the game, for example, hug, mug, bug and lug. Amrit begins the game by saying, "I am thinking of a word that rhymes with hug."

The rest of the players ask questions to help them guess the target word.

For example, Margot might ask, "Is it something that is eaten by a spider?"

Amrit must then reply, guessing the word that Margot was thinking of when she asked the question: "No, Margot, it's not a bug."

Or, "Is it something you drink coffee out of?" "No, it's not a mug."

If Margot asks a question for which Amrit cannot find a rhyming answer, he is considered "stumped." For example, Margot may ask, "Is it something that pulls other boats around the harbor?" If Amrit cannot say, "No, it's not a tug," then Amrit is out and Margot gets to choose the next word.

Similarly, if Margot says, "Is it something you put on your floor and vacuum?" she has guessed the word correctly and gets to choose the next word.

VARIATIONS

See Dumb Crambo for a variation that does not allow the guessing players to speak and instead requires them to act out the answers.

MODIFICATIONS

To decrease the difficulty level, allow the player with the target word (Amrit) more than one chance if he is stumped by the questions from the guessing player (Margot).

NOTE Make sure the questions being asked by the guessing players aren't too vague. If Margot asks, "Is it something you buy in a store?" the answers could be almost unlimited. Try not to eliminate a player because of a vague question; instead, ask them to be more specific.

Lost for Words

Some of your participants may need extra assistance for word and brain games such as Crambo, I Spy and Twenty Questions. You can help kids with memory challenges or limited vocabularies and also those who are shy about speaking in front of others by:

- Picking a word or phrase or question out of a hat,
- Coaching by whispering,
- Having the child whisper the word or phrase he or she chooses to the leader, so the leader can play as a partner,
- Having or helping the child draw the word, or
- Brainstorming a list of questions, words or phrases before the game begins.

  The best adaptations are often those that do not single out any one participant but help the entire group.

Dumb Crambo

PLAYERS 4 or more

EQUIPMENT None

GAME PLAN Guess the target word through a series of rhyming words and charades.

HOW TO PLAY

Divide the group into two even teams: the actors and the rhymers.

Have the actors leave the group while the rhymers either decide on or are told the target word that the actors must guess. Once the rhymers agree on their target word and think of several words that rhyme with their target word, they can call back the actors.

The rhymers then tell the actors a word that rhymes with their target word. For example, if the target word is "hour," the rhymers might say, "We are thinking of a word that rhymes with power."

The actors have 10 seconds to decide which word they will begin acting out. If the actors think the word might be "tower," they would mime building a tower, or stand as straight as towers, or pretend to be Rapunzel in a tower.

The rhymers must figure out what the mime is and respond, "No it's not a tower."

The actors might then mime a growing garden, or smelling beautiful roses. The rhymers would then respond, "No, it's not a flower."

If the actors move to create a giant ticking clock, that means they have hit on the word, and the rhymers would respond, "Yes, it's an hour!"

The rhymers and the actors then switch roles, and points are awarded to the actors based on how many guesses the actors took to act out the target word.

If the rhymers cannot guess the mime, and you think the mime is correct (for example, an hour-glass or someone repeatedly checking her watch), then you can award points to the actors.

VARIATIONS

Dumb Crambo can be played individually rather than on teams by following the procedures for individual Charades or individual Pictionary (see pages 39–41).

See Crambo (page 51) for a similar game that doesn't involve acting out the answers.

MODIFICATIONS

To increase the difficulty, allow the actors only five seconds for consultation, or no time at all.

To modify the difficulty level either up or down, choose either difficult or easy to rhyme words instead of letting players pick their own words.

Look Up, Look Down

PLAYERS 8 and up

EQUIPMENT None

GAME PLAN Avoid looking at someone who is looking at you!

HOW TO PLAY

Have players stand in a circle, with everyone looking down at their feet.

On the command "Look up," all players must look up into the eyes of another player in the circle – they do not have to be directly across, just someone in the circle.

If that person happens to be looking back, both players must point at each other and let out a loud scream before sitting on the floor, eliminated from the game.

After everyone who is eliminated sits down, call "Look down," and start again from the beginning.

The winner is the last person (or last two people) standing, depending on whether the total number of participants is odd or even.

NOTE Watch for cheaters! Often players will start by looking in one place and then look in another. If you find you're dealing with a group of cheaters, consider implementing a look-and-point rule.

Heads Up, Seven Up

PLAYERS Best with 15 or more

EQUIPMENT None

GAME PLAN Discover which player of seven tapped your head.

HOW TO PLAY

Choose seven players to stand in front of the other players, who are all seated together (with enough space to walk between everyone).

Have all remaining players put their heads down, covering their eyes. Make sure nobody is peeking!

Then have the chosen seven players walk in between the other players, choosing one each to tap (lightly) on the head, and return to the front.

Once players have been tapped on the head, they must put a hand up in the air (but keep their eyes closed!) so they don't get double-tapped.

Once all seven players have tapped one person each, they return to the front and say, "Heads Up, Seven Up."

The rest of the group will then have one try to guess which person tapped their heads. If they guess correctly, they switch places with the players at the front. If they guess incorrectly, they must remain seated.

After everyone has guessed, those at the front who were not correctly identified reveal which person they touched, but get to remain up at the front for the next round.

MODIFICATIONS

If there are fewer people, change the name to "Heads Up, Five Up," or whatever number applies.

DRAMA GAMES

These games are all at home in drama classrooms and studios. While many of them require some degree of acting and performance skill, others are in this section because of their emphasis on quick reflexes, teamwork, and listening to and watching your fellow players — skills that are important for any budding actor or actress to develop.

Look for the magic wand throughout the book if you're interested in other drama-inspired games that rely on make-believe or performance.

Broken Telephone

PLAYERS 8 or more

EQUIPMENT None

GAME PLAN Pass a phrase down the line of players without muddying the message.

HOW TO PLAY

Have the players sit in a circle. Think of a word or phrase to whisper in a player's ear. Choose your phrase according to the age of your campers. For five-year-olds, "hot dogs are yummy with mustard" is of a challenging length, but contains familiar words. For 12-year-olds, "swiss, mozzarella, cheddar and gouda are types of cheese that make me drool-a" is longer, more complicated and contains a play on words.

Whisper the phrase to the player on your left while cupping your hand to their ear. That player then whispers the phrase to the player on his left, who whispers it to the player on her left, and so on. When the phrase reaches the last player in the circle, that player says it out loud. "Hot dogs are yummy with mustard" may have become "Long hogs are funny and dusty."

If the player receiving the message thought that the message was too quiet or poorly mumbled, she is entitled to one "Operator" call, where the talking player has to repeat the message at a slightly louder volume. This rule is helpful but can slow the game down, so use it sparingly.

VARIATIONS

With older players, have them write suggested messages on scraps of paper. This way you can control the content of the messages. With particularly saucy groups of older players, we have found that Broken Telephone can easily wander into PG-13 territory, so some monitoring may be required.

For a variation that tests your players' speed and accuracy, have a Broken Telephone race. Divide the teams up into two and have them line up facing each other. Whisper the initial message to the players at the start of each line and have them whisper the message down the line. Give points for fastest message and most accurate message.

Who's the Leader?

PLAYERS 8 or more

EQUIPMENT None

GAME PLAN Discover the leader of the secret rhythm or protect the leader of the secret rhythm.

HOW TO PLAY

Have players sit or stand in a circle. Choose one player to be the Rhythm Breaker and have him leave the circle and stand with his back facing the circle, behind a tree, or just outside the door.

Choose one player to be the Rhythm Leader. Make sure that everybody else in the circle knows who the Rhythm Leader is.

Have the Rhythm Leader begin a simple rhythm or movement, and tell the group to follow the leader.

Suggested actions include marching on the spot, tapping feet, snapping fingers, rubbing tummy, sticking tongue out, and making circles with hands.

When the rhythm has been established, call the Breaker back and have him stand in the middle. When the Breaker's back is turned, the Leader can change up her pattern to a different rhythm or movement.

The Breaker should be able to detect the change in sound and pace and figure out who the Leader is. The Breaker gets two chances to guess who the Rhythm Leader is before the Leader can claim victory and take her place as the next Breaker.

You can force the Breaker to make guesses after every two changes of rhythm, and alternately you can oust a Leader who refuses to change the rhythm.

NOTE Encourage the other players not to look directly at the Leader when the Breaker comes back, as direct eye-contact with the Leader might tip off the Breaker.

VARIATIONS

A noncompetitive version of this game is called Everybody Is the Leader. In this variation, all players stand in the circle, facing each other. One person starts off with a rhythm or movement, and the rest of the group follows. Without talking, a different group member assumes leadership and changes the rhythm, and the rest of the group follows. In this variation, leadership should flow naturally between the different members of the group so there is no fighting over who gets to decide the next move.

Human Machine

PLAYERS Any number

EQUIPMENT None

GAME PLAN Form a human machine to resemble a real machine.

HOW TO PLAY

Divide players into even teams of at least four to five players. If you have fewer players, or if you are looking for an extra challenge with a large group, consider having one group.

Go round to each group and whisper a type of machine that the players should be familiar with. Examples could include a hole puncher, a pasta or sausage maker, a bicycle, a laundry machine, a computer or television, a car, a boat, a sewing machine, a stapler, a vending machine and a toilet.

Each group has five minutes to figure out all the parts of their machine, and assign roles. For example, if your group was a hole-puncher, three people could be the punchers, and one person could be the piece of paper. The groups should practice making the machines "work," complete with sound effects.

The groups present their machines and the other groups can guess what type of machine they were. Points can be awarded for creativity, sound effects and correct guessing.

Red Ball, Yellow Ball

PLAYERS Any number

EQUIPMENT None

GAME PLAN Learn everyone's name and simultaneously catch and throw imaginary balls of different colors and sizes.

HOW TO PLAY

Have the group stand in a circle. Hold your hands out as if you were holding a baseball. Say to the group, "This is a red ball," and have them approximate the size of the red ball with their hands.

Pick one player to throw the imaginary ball to – for example – Keegan. When you throw the ball to Keegan, you say, "Red ball Keegan." When Keegan catches the ball, he says, "Red ball thank you." Keegan then throws the ball to Denver, saying, "Red ball Denver," and so on.

After the group has mastered the small red ball, introduce a medium-sized yellow ball. Both balls should be in circulation at the same time. This increases the difficulty level and concentration required to both remember what size of imaginary ball you are holding, and to listen for your name to be called so you can catch the ball.

This game is a good ice-breaker. For others, see Break the Ice, starting at page 15.

VARIATIONS

Vary your throwing technique and speed, effort required, weight, size and number of balls in the air to increase the level of difficulty. It is tempting to play this game with elimination, but we caution against it because of the challenge of evaluating whether a ball is dropped or properly sized.

MODIFICATIONS

For groups that find mime tricky, try playing this game with real balls first. You could also play a simple game of a Catch (page 88) to remind the players of what the motions of throwing and catching look like.

Master and Servant

PLAYERS Any number, but better with 15 or more

EQUIPMENT Enough chairs for just fewer than half of your players to sit down

GAME PLAN Escape your wicked master, or keep your servant in his place.

HOW TO PLAY

Have the group arrange the chairs in a circle, facing inward. Have more than half your players stand 2 feet behind the chairs, with their hands behind their backs: they are the Masters. Have the remaining players sit in the chairs with their backs against the chair-back: they are the Servants. For example, if you have 15 players, have 9 Masters and 6 Servants, with three remaining open chairs. If you have 25 players, have 15 Masters, 10 Servants and five open chairs.

Tell your group that the Masters with open chairs and without Servants in front of them are lazy and want to get some help around the house. To do so, they must make eye contact with and wink at a Servant across the circle. The winked-at Servant must then try to escape his existing Master and run to the new Master with the empty chair, where he will then become the new Master's Servant.

The Servant must move toward the empty chair within five seconds of being winked at, but if the existing Master sees the winking or catches the Servant beginning to run away, she can reach out and tap her Servant on the shoulder. The Servant is then caught and must sit down until another Master winks at him.

To increase the speed of play and difficulty level, a Servant can "psych out" his existing Master by jerking forward in his seat. If the Master taps the Servant when the Servant was not actually trying to escape, the Master and Servant switch places.

MODIFICATIONS

For players who cannot wink, have Masters stick their tongues out to call the Servants.

Improv Games

Improv — short for improvisation — is a type of drama that is always unscripted and, more often than not, hilarious. The idea behind these games may seem simple: create a scene based on a few simple prompts, and develop characters, settings, problems and solutions to fit that scene. However, these games require lots of creativity, on-the-spot thinking and communication skills.

There are even tournaments and competitions where skilled groups of improv players get together to compete. At these competitions, points are awarded for originality, dramatic interest and teamwork. Improv games tend to be more successful with participants ages ten and up because of the planning and story-telling skills required. Here are some general rules that apply to all improv games:

- Role model the first round of all these games with a leader or another capable participant.

- Don't say no. Your teammate may come up with a ridiculous idea or say something absurd, but once it is a part of the scene, you can't say no to it. For example, your teammate might say, "Your pants are on fire!" Don't say, "No, they aren't." Instead respond "Yikes! Help me put them out!" before promptly dropping to the ground and rolling.

- Don't say yes too easily. Drama is about conflict. If the scene is about whether or not Junior can go to the mall with his friends, Mom should not immediately agree. Instead, she should bring up Junior's refusal to take his dog for a walk, his lack of money and the fact that he has to babysit his younger sister. Junior could then convince Mom to let him go by promising to buy her the pair of boxing gloves she's always wanted.

- Don't leave the scene. As soon as one partner leaves the scene, it is over.

- When the scene starts to die, or you have solved the problem presented in the scene, one or all of the players should shout, "Scene!" If the scene starts to die, the leader can wrap it up by making a twirling motion with his hands and encouraging them to finish quickly, or by calling "Scene!" for the players.

- A tip for choosing scenarios: Kids will want to play scenes on the moon, on airplanes and under the sea, but it is often easier for them to come up with ideas if they are make-believing in a familiar environment. Scenes about whose turn it is to take out the garbage can be funnier than scenes about space-monkeys from Mars.

Freeze

PLAYERS Any number

EQUIPMENT None

GAME PLAN Create a brief scene before being "frozen" and replaced by an incoming actor.

HOW TO PLAY

Seat the players as an audience in front of the "stage" and pick two actors to start. Ask the actors to imagine that they are swimming through Jell-O. When they are in an interesting position, shout "Freeze."

The actors must then start a scene about anything, preferably about something that relates to their body position. For example, if Samuel was reaching up when the scene started, he might ask Sapna to help him get the cookie jar off the top shelf. Sapna might then say, "No! Mom'll catch us and we're not supposed to have cookies before dinner."

If an audience member sees one of the actors move in an interesting way, they can call "Freeze" to pause the scene. The audience member goes up on stage, taps one of the actors on the shoulder, and assumes that actor's position. The new audience member must then start a different scene using the same position. For example, Victoria might tap out the reaching Samuel from the cookie scene and start a scene about playing basketball.

We like to encourage participants to wait 30 seconds before calling "Freeze," and to wait until three or four other people have gone up instead of calling "Freeze" several times in a row.

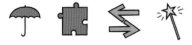

Bus Stop/Park Bench

PLAYERS Any number

EQUIPMENT A few chairs or a bench

GAME PLAN Wait for a bus and then find a reason to walk instead, or try to convince someone to give up their spot on the park bench.

HOW TO PLAY

Seat the players as an audience in front of the bench. Ask all the players to think of a zany character and pick two actors to start.

The basic premise of both Bus Stop and Park Bench is that one player starts on the bench, another player enters, and they interact with each other. One thing leads to another, and the first character finds a reason to leave the scene, leaving the second player alone. The leader should then pick a third actor to enter the scene.

The main difference between Bus Stop and Park Bench is in the reason for being on the bench in the first place.

In Bus Stop, the character on the bench is waiting for a bus. He is not allowed to check his watch or ask when the bus is supposed to come. He must find a reason to leave the scene and walk instead.

For example, Graham sits on the bench. His character is an executive who is late for a meeting at work and whose car is in the shop. Michelle enters as a cat-lady who brings on five imaginary cats that she is taking to the veterinarian. The two trade pleasantries, but when Michelle offers Graham one of her cats to pet, he has a sneezing fit and runs offstage to fetch a doctor. The leader then picks another player to go up – for example, Fizza, who walks on with an imaginary dog that scares off all of Michelle's imaginary cats.

In Park Bench, the goal of both characters is to enjoy the prime location of the park bench. The characters must persuade the other character to give up the park bench, either through bribery, bullying, freaky behavior or some other strategy.

For example, grumpy Joshua is dozing in the sun on his favorite park bench, when cheery Luciana walks up and sees that her favorite bench is occupied. She sidles up to him, giggling and making small talk, aggravating him so much that he asks her to leave the bench. Then Luciana's giggles turn into sobs, so Joshua leaves to go find peace and quiet somewhere else.

Of course, these scenarios are only suggestions: you and your budding actors will be able to come up with a variety of ideas.

Sitting, Standing, Lying

PLAYERS Any number

EQUIPMENT None required, but a chair or a bench are useful

GAME PLAN Perform a scene where one actor is always sitting, one is standing, and one is lying down.

HOW TO PLAY

Set up the furniture (if using) "on stage" and seat the audience. Give the three actors a conflict that will help them begin the scene. Suggested conflicts include making dinner, taking the dog for a walk, getting a failing report card, fixing the kitchen sink or bullying a friend.

The performers begin the scene, attempting to solve the conflict in an interesting, funny fashion. However, at all times, one player must be sitting down (on the chair or ground), one player must be lying down (on the table or the ground), and one player must be standing.

Players should find a way to integrate the changes in movement into their dialogue. For example, if Peter gets fed up fixing the sink, he could sit down in frustration. When Mira goes to turn the tap, she could be sprayed with a flow of water that knocks her down into the lying position. Whenever the scene gets boring, a player can change position to force his fellow actors to react.

Shy Kids

A few simple tips will help you make the experience more positive for shy kids.

- Often in drama games we pick partners randomly to encourage the group to work with a variety of partners. It is better to pair shy kids with their existing, preferably outgoing friends. Pair a shy kid with a good listener who can wait for his shy scene partner to say something before moving the scene forward.

- Talk privately to the shy kid's scene partner before they go up on stage. Encourage the partner to ask open-ended questions to their shy partner.

- Be the shy kid's partner yourself.

Party Quirks

PLAYERS Any number

EQUIPMENT None

GAME PLAN Host or attend a party with some quirky characters and guess what the character's quirks are.

HOW TO PLAY

Seat the players as an audience in front of your "stage" and pick four actors to start. One actor, Colin, is the host of the party. Take the other three actors aside and give them unique quirks that will influence the way that they walk, talk and interact with the other players. Some examples include police officer, fortune teller, kindergarten teacher, surfer, weather forecaster, guy who can talk to animals, and girl whose pants are on fire.

The scene begins with Colin getting his house ready for the party, when a doorbell rings. The first guest could be a supermodel: she comes in the door and begins to strut her stuff while Colin invites her to help herself to some chips. After about 30 seconds, the doorbell rings and Colin invites in the second guest, a home-improvement television show host. After another 30 seconds, the third character arrives.

As soon as the second character arrives, Colin can begin to guess their "quirks." Instead of breaking character and asking directly, he should do this through dialogue: "Okay home-improvement guy, this is a party, not a TV show." The characters at the party should interact with each other. For example, the supermodel can ask the home-improvement expert to build her a runway.

Once their quirk has been guessed, the actor should leave the stage. Once the host has guessed all the quirks, the party is over and a new set of actors is chosen.

Murder Wink

PLAYERS 6 or more

EQUIPMENT None

GAME PLAN Find the murderer.

HOW TO PLAY

Have the players sit in a circle.

Pick one player to be the Detective and have her turn away from the group or go behind a tree. Ask the rest of the players close their eyes.

Stand up and pat a different player on the head: he is the Murderer.

Tell the players to open their eyes and have the Detective come back to the group and stand in the middle of the circle.

When the Murderer is ready, he can begin winking at other members of the group.

If a player has been winked at, he or she has to melodramatically pretend to die (for example, making gagging noises, screaming, etc.) and fall over.

The Detective must try to stop the murders from happening by guessing who the Murderer is. The Detective has three guesses. If she has not figured it out by the third guess, the Murderer is triumphant and becomes the Detective for the next round.

Consider changing the number of guesses a Detective has according to the number of players in the game. For example, with fewer than 8 players, two guesses will probably suffice.

VARIATIONS

You can call the game Celebrity Wink, and the player patted on the head becomes a celebrity who winks at his adoring fans. Players winked at fall into a swoon.

To keep the game rated G, call the game "Sleepy Wink" and have the players fall asleep instead.

MODIFICATIONS

If you have children who are unable to wink, tell them they can stick their tongues out.

Up, Jenkins!

PLAYERS 6 or more

EQUIPMENT A coin and a table

GAME PLAN Guess who has the coin.

HOW TO PLAY

Divide the group into two teams and seat them either in a line facing each other or preferably on either side of a table.

Choose a leader for both teams – Leanne and Natalie, for example. Pick one team to start.

If Natalie's team starts with the coin, they pass it back and forth with their hands underneath the table. While this is happening, Leanne counts slowly to 10 and calls, "Up, Jenkins!" All players on Natalie's team must raise their fists in the air above the table.

Natalie then calls, "Down, Jenkins!" All the players on her team slam their fists on the table, opening their palms and – they hope – keeping the coin concealed. Leanne's team should keep their eyes and ears open in case the coin slips out or makes a chinging noise as it comes down to the table.

Leanne and her team consult for 10 seconds (Natalie can count the time) and then call the name of the player on Natalie's team who they think has the coin.

The called-out player must raise his hands off the table to reveal whether or not he has hidden the coin.

Depending on the number of players and the desired difficulty level, you can decide how many guesses Leanne's team gets: for large groups, you might allow as many as four or five guesses, but for teams of only three or four, you might only allow one or two guesses. You can switch after each round, or after each time the guess is successful.

Alternatively, you can use a low score system, where each guess a team makes counts against them. For example, if Leanne's team took three guesses to figure out who had the coin, they get three points. If Natalie's team only took one guess to figure out who had the coin, they get one point. The team with the lowest number of points then wins.

VARIATIONS

If there is no table to be found, players can sit cross-legged across from each other and pass the coin behind their backs.

MODIFICATIONS

If your group has shy players, have them take turns being the team leader: this game does not require much actual leadership skill, but it can be a great confidence boost for someone who has never been a leader before.

To increase the difficulty level, have players guess which hand the coin is under.

Electricity

PLAYERS 8 or more

EQUIPMENT None

GAME PLAN Keep the electricity flowing, or guess where it is hidden.

HOW TO PLAY

Have the group sit or stand in a circle and hold hands.

Explain to the group that we have electricity in our body that helps us move. Practice passing electricity around the circle by squeezing each other's hands. For example, if Sammy squeezes Julie's hand, and Julie squeezes Timothy's hand, the electricity passes from Sammy to Julie to Timothy.

Pick one player to be the electrician. She must sit or stand in the middle of the circle.

Explain to the group that the electrical wiring has gone crazy, and that this electrician needs to stop it before a power meltdown hits. She has to track down the source of the wacky electricity. The electrician must close her eyes and count to 10 before trying to figure out where the electricity is.

The job of the group is to pass the electricity around the circle stealthily so that when the electrician opens her eyes, she cannot guess who has the electricity.

The job of the electrician is to watch the group's facial expressions and hands to look for a sign of a squeeze.

Any player caught squeezing falsely will not be allowed to be the electrician!

Although most players try to go as quickly as possible, remind them that a slow-moving electric wave is stealthier than a quickly moving one.

The electrician has three chances (depending on the size of the group) to guess where the electricity is. If she points to where the electricity is, the caught person is then be the electrician. If she runs out of guesses, she is "stumped" and the leader picks a new electrician.

VARIATIONS

For a simpler version of the game, instead of having players squeeze each others' hands, have them pass an item around their backs. Play Doggy Doggy (see also page 86) and use this rhyme:

"Doggy, Doggy, who's got your bone? Somebody stole it from your home. Guess who, maybe you. Or maybe the monkey from the zoo. So wake up, Doggy, find your bone. If you find it, take it home!"

When the rhyme ends the bone stops and the Doggy, who is sitting in the middle of the circle with eyes closed, "wakes up" and has to find his bone.

MODIFICATIONS

To increase the difficulty, have players cross their arms. Or, have a "double squeeze" that sends the squeeze back to the direction it came from.

Also Known As (AKA)

Many of the games in this book are known by other names. In your part of the world, you may know King's Keys as Pirate's Treasure. Soh Koh No is also known as Ah Soh Koh. Some games that sound the same, aren't: there are at least four games in this book that have Sharks in the name, each with a thrilling bite but each a little bit different. And we have our own version of Octopus that we call Run Like Chewbacca.

Then there are all the local variations in the rules! Where we know good alternate names and ways of playing games, we have tried to include them. Undoubtedly we have missed some of your favorites. We hope you'll continue to play those, but also find plenty of new inspiration and maybe learn some new tricks for playing old standards in these pages.

King's Keys
(aka Pirate's Treasure)

PLAYERS 5 or more

EQUIPMENT Any small object that can make a sound, such as keys or a rattle.

GAME PLAN Steal the keys from the King without getting caught.

HOW TO PLAY

Have the group sit in a circle and choose one player to sit in the middle of the circle with a blindfold on or eyes closed. That player is the King (or Queen, or Pirate). Near the King is an object, usually one that will make a sound when moved.

Pick another player from the circle to quietly sneak into the circle and try to steal the object from the King.

The King has to listen for noises and point in the direction he thinks the noise is coming from. If he points at the sneaking player, she has to return to her spot in the circle. Keep picking children to try until the keys are stolen. The successful thief becomes the new King.

VARIATIONS

This game can also be played as Pirate's Treasure.

If more kids are playing, add more objects. Even a piece of paper will work. The King or Pirate can get out only when all the objects have been stolen, and then the game is over.

MODIFICATIONS

Often, players trying to steal can get uppity about "being pointed at," and will insist they weren't pointed at. If you have stubborn players like this, instead of the King "pointing," equip him with some soft foam balls or beanbags to toss in the direction he believes the thief is coming from. If the thief is hit, she must return to her spot.

Soh Koh No
(aka Ah Soh Ko)

PLAYERS 6 or more

EQUIPMENT None

GAME PLAN Pass the "ch'i" energy around the circle.

HOW TO PLAY

All the players sit together in a circle. The leader will explain to them the traditional Chinese concept of ch'i – which is, in a nutshell, energy that flows through our homes, lives and self.

The players must learn how to properly direct the ch'i around the circle. There are two ways of doing this: Soh! (always said with energy) is when the player directs the energy to either side of her, arms facing opposite directions, palms facing inward. The direction of the bottom hand is the direction in which the energy is traveling.

If the player wants to transfer the ch'i to someone not directly beside them, they must say Koh!, pointing with both hands directly at the intended recipient.

Players have to respond to the energy directed at them. They have the option to reject the energy, but only if it has been delivered to them through a Koh! To reject the ch'i, players must say No! bringing their arms into and then out of an "X" shape in front of their torso.

This game can be quite challenging when you keep in mind the following complications: you cannot begin a round with a Koh!, and you cannot No! a Soh! You can, however, alternate direction with Soh! at any time by changing the direction your bottom hand is pointing.

Players are eliminated if they break either of the preceding rules, or if they mistakenly think the ch'i was directed toward them, and begin to redirect it.

Veteran players often try and psych out other players by looking to their right while saying Soh!, but with their bottom hand directing the ch'i toward their left, or vice versa; this is a quick way to eliminate those on either side of you.

To increase the difficulty level, have eliminated players remain in the circle. Remaining players will be eliminated if they Koh the ch'i to a person who is out or if they do not accept a Soh! and are the active player to the right or left, or if they Koh! to a player who is the active player to their right or left (this may be despite having several eliminated players in between).

VARIATIONS

Some camps have a version of this game called Ah Soh Koh. Players must follow the order Ah!-Soh!-Koh!

The first player says Ah! and with one hand held palm down, arm at shoulder height, points right

or left to the player next to them. That player must declare Soh! and, raising one arm above his head, point to one side or the other; the person he points at must say Koh! and hold both hands together in front, pointing at another player anywhere in the circle.

When they are pointed at, players must respond with another action. When Koh'd, they can start again with Ah or put their hands up and say No! If players make the wrong motion or miss their action, they are eliminated and have to step out of the circle.

MODIFICATIONS

Hearing- and language-challenged players should be able to fully participate as long as the gestures are clear and consistent.

To make the game more challenging (and noisier), you can have eliminated players walk around outside the circle shouting out words to try to confuse the remaining players — but use this option with discretion, deciding if your group can handle this extra element responsibly.

If you like Soh Koh No, try playing Ford Angular Gear Box, the Wild West version of this game (page 83).

NOTE We realize this seems overwhelming, but it is one of our favorite games. Consult the illustrations and try it!

Dictionary

PLAYERS Any number

EQUIPMENT A dictionary, pencils and small pieces of paper

GAME PLAN Create a misleading, fake definition of a strange word and guess the correct dictionary definition of the word.

HOW TO PLAY

This game works best when most or all of the players can read and write. Divide the players into even teams. More than five teams is difficult for scorekeeping. Give each of the teams several pieces of paper and a pencil.

Open the dictionary and look for a word that the players most likely will not know: for example, "elucidate," which means to make clear and more understandable. Ask each team to write down a definition for "elucidate" on their piece of paper. The definition does not have to actually be accurate; rather, it should be something that could be the definition. For example, a team could write that "elucidate" also means "an

unlucky date," or "a day that you forgot happened," or "a rare fruit found in the wilds of Canada."

Write down the actual definition on a slip of paper and collect the papers from the groups. Read all the definitions out loud and ask the groups to guess which definition is the correct definition. You may have to reread the definitions several times before groups will feel confident guessing their definition.

Points are awarded for groups that guess the correct definition, as well as groups whose definition is guessed by others. For example, if Claire's group wrote down "an unlucky date" as their definition, and Supreet's group guesses "an unlucky date" as the correct definition, Claire's group wins a point. If, on the other hand, Supreet's group guesses that elucidate means "to make clear," then they win a point.

VARIATIONS

For theme days, you can plan ahead and research words that are related to your theme — all science words or all medieval words, for example.

MODIFICATIONS

For age groups that have begun learning to read and write, but have not mastered the "dictionary" style, be sure that the real definition is written in a language that they will understand. For "elucidate," you might write "to help someone understand" instead of "to make clear or manifest."

Bop!

PLAYERS 6 or more

EQUIPMENT None

GAME PLAN Stay in the game by avoiding the temptation to say "Bop" at the wrong time ... but making sure to say it at the right time!

HOW TO PLAY

Have the players stand in a circle.

Choose one player — for example, Sarah — to stand in the middle and be It.

Sarah must go around the circle saying "Bop" to the other players. In response, they must stay silent. However, if Sarah says "Bop–diddly-op-bop," the player being spoken to must say "Bop" before Sarah has finished speaking. Otherwise, that player is eliminated and has to sit down.

This game is more challenging than it seems!

VARIATIONS

Bop can be played together with Speed Rabbit (see page 77).

Dealing with Rule Breakers

Children break rules for two simple reasons: they either don't understand the game, or they aren't winning.

For children who don't understand the game, practice rounds should help. Try explaining the rules for the game each time the group plays it. Demonstrate the wrong way, and then have the rule breaker demonstrate the right way. This method of demonstration is particularly useful with complicated rules such as offside. Demonstration and hands-on practice is also very important for children with attention or memory difficulties.

Additionally, some rules just take time to get into our muscle memory. For example, seasoned soccer players know never to grab the ball with their hands. However, we amateurs will inevitably respond to having a soccer ball thrown at our heads by pulling our hands up to our face to block the ball.

Treat this type of rule breaker gently and with encouragement. Praise your players when they remember the proper rules or procedures, and avoid over-criticizing them when they break the rules.

The second type of rule breaker is more challenging. These are often children who are highly competitive and can be sore losers. If a game isn't going in their favor, they will purposely break a rule because they would rather break a rule than be known as a bad player or a loser.

For example, if Jesse has been bragging all week about how good he is at Duck, Duck, Goose (see page 91), and then he loses his seat twice in a row, he might body-check the next player he goes up against instead of losing a third time. Jesse would rather be told off by a leader for body-checking a fellow player than have his other group members see that he isn't as good at Duck, Duck, Goose as he's been saying. Fear of losing the game is the reason many professional athletes take penalties.

We recommend that you treat this type of rule-breaker the same way professional athletes are treated: give him a short time out (you can call it a penalty for older kids, who will understand the idea of penalty minutes), explain what he did wrong, and let him back into the game. You can give out penalty minutes relative to the age of the camper and the offense. You might also have him forfeit his turn in the game, depending on what type of game you are playing (for example, for Duck, Duck, Goose, Jesse would have to sit down and wouldn't be It anymore).

After the game, ask him if he can remember why he chose to break the rule. You might ask him why the rule is there in the first place (for instance, to keep people safe, to keep the game running smoothly). Praise him for his good efforts in the game, but remind him that playing by the rules is part of being an athlete, a teammate and a friend.

Silent Ball

PLAYERS 5 or more

EQUIPMENT A medium-sized ball

GAME PLAN A simple game of catch tweaked to settle down a group.

HOW TO PLAY

Have the players sit in a circle. Encourage the players to make as much noise as possible before the game, but explain that during the game, they must be completely silent.

Have the players yell for 10 seconds and then say, "The silence begins... now!" The players must then be quiet and pass the ball to each other around the circle.

If the pass is thrown poorly, and the receiver misses, the passer is out. If the pass was good, and the receiver misses, the receiver is out.

Players may not pass to their neighbors until there are only four players left.

If anyone makes a sound, he or she is out. Players are allowed to breathe, sneeze and cough, but are not allowed to say anything, including "Rats" or "Pass the ball over here!"

Play until everyone is out or the game is peaked.

Penalty minutes, however, are not appropriate at all times. Depending on the offense, you might instead have a change-over in possession of a ball, an extra point for another team, or simply a warning.

You should use penalty minutes sparingly with children who are hesitant to get involved at all. If Betsy doesn't want to play Red Light, Green Light (see page 116) and makes that known by standing still at the starting line, giving her a time out or a penalty will not encourage her to participate. Instead, perhaps have her be the caller, or make it a three-legged Red Light, Green Light so that she can feel that she is a part of the group.

Finally, if you are playing a game of Frozen Tag (page 121), and suddenly the whole group stops freezing and breaks all the rules, the children are probably bored stiff and breaking the rules to add some excitement. In that case, it is time to move on to a new game.

Scavenger Hunt

PLAYERS Any number

EQUIPMENT Paper, pen, bag(s)

GAME PLAN Find all the objects on a given list.

HOW TO PLAY
Gather the group together and hand out the list of items they need to collect. For example, your list could include three pine cones, a red maple leaf, a plastic bag, a flat rock and an acorn.

If the group requires constant supervision (or you are searching a large, perhaps unknown area open to the public), go with the group and help them in their search for the items on the list.

You can time the "hunt" to give additional motivation.

If your area is more private and the players are old enough to be trusted alone, send them off in small groups to compete against each other to collect all the items first.

MODIFICATIONS
For a small group with more independent participants, try giving each player a personal list to hunt for.

Backwards Scavenger Hunt

PLAYERS Any number

EQUIPMENT Paper, pen, bag(s)

GAME PLAN Find a certain number of objects...and hope they're on the scavenger hunt list.

HOW TO PLAY
This game is like Scavenger Hunt (above), except backwards!

Announce to the players how many items you have on your hidden list of items, which you will have created ahead of time. (The items should be objects readily available in your area.)

Send players around an area to collect a certain number of items, to match the number of items on your hidden list. Players will have an allotted amount of time to collect items that they think are on your list.

When the time is up, players must return with their items. Then you will run through your list with them. Every time the group has an item that was on the list, they receive a point.

If there are several groups, the group with the most points wins.

Blow Soccer

PLAYERS 6 or fewer. Otherwise, play with rotations or multiple fields

EQUIPMENT A ping pong ball, straws and chalk

GAME PLAN Simulate a large-scale soccer game on the smallest field possible.

HOW TO PLAY

Divide the teams up evenly. Distribute a straw to each player. (For sanitary reasons, do not share straws.)

With chalk, draw the outlines of a soccer field, including goal posts, on a floor, on a table, or on a piece of Bristol board or chart paper. We recommend that the "field" be about 2 feet wide by 3 feet long, or approximately the size of a piece of Bristol board.

Set up the players around the field, ensuring that each team has someone to tend goal and play defense, and someone to play offense.

Depending on the number of players, you might want to institute a "no shuffling" rule, which means that players cannot move their knees from their initial position.

Place the ping pong ball at center field and start with a face-off. Pushing their breath through the straws, players control the movement of the ping pong ball and attempt to score in their opponent's net. While there is some strategy involved, for the large part, this game is dependent on the luck of who needs to breathe when.

Follow the rules of soccer in terms of out-of-bound throw-ins versus corner kick possessions and "hands-free" play. Any player who touches the ping pong ball with a hand forfeits possession to the other team for a penalty blow.

VARIATIONS

This game can also be played on a miniature hockey rink or on a ping pong table without the nets.

MODIFICATIONS

Position the game on a table for players who have difficulty getting low to the ground. Use larger straws, or allow children with poor breath control to "poke" the ball with the straw rather than blow it.

OVERNIGHT CAMP

While the games in this book work well for day camps, recreation programs, classrooms and backyards, the games and activities in this section are designed with a particular type of camp in mind: overnight, or sleep-away camp. As leaders of day camp programs, we were always envious of the authenticity of overnight camps: that was where we suspected "real" camping happened.

The main strength of overnight camp (aside from being able to actually go camping — something that doesn't happen in community centers) is that the time apart from the outside world gives both leaders and campers a chance to develop real friendships and relationships based on trust and shared adventures, which is different from the social networks that tend to develop at schools. Here, campers are not evaluated based on how well they did on last week's geography test, or whether their clothes are the "right" labels. Everyone is too busy playing with real geography and dirtying their clothes to care what label they are!

A Little Night Music

PLAYERS Any number

EQUIPMENT None

GAME PLAN Identify the different noisemakers of the night and create your own soundtrack.

HOW TO PLAY

Begin by discussing how the night sounds are their own little orchestra. Tell players to listen for all the noises the night makes. You might hear frogs, birds, crickets, waves, wind, a campfire.

Ask all of the players to pick a night sound to make: Rebecca is a frog, Vicki is the wind and Jeffrey is a cricket, for example. As the leader, you might want to be a sound that occurs frequently and rhythmically – we like to be the waves, so we can keep the beat.

Tell the players that they are going to make a song, just like the night sounds. Begin by keeping the beat with the waves and point to players to get them to jump in one at a time. You can conduct your night orchestra with hand gestures – get certain group members to make their noises more often or less often, louder or quieter. After a few minutes, you can slow down the music and point players out, until all you are left with is the real night music.

Feelings on the Floor

PLAYERS Any number, but best with under 10

EQUIPMENT A number of index card-sized pieces of paper with emotions written on them

GAME PLAN Choose from a pile of feelings on the floor to express how you are feeling.

HOW TO PLAY

To prepare for this game, write a bunch of feelings that your participants might be experiencing: anxious, excited, afraid, happy, frustrated, joyful, confused, exhausted and enthusiastic are just a few examples. You can have more than one copy of the same feeling.

Throw the feeling cards on the floor and invite each player to pick up a card that describes best what they are feeling right then. Then invite each player to share why they are feeling that way.

If participants tend to choose the same feelings every time you play this game, remove that feeling card from the pile so that they can broaden their perspective.

Star Pictures

PLAYERS Any number

EQUIPMENT A night sky filled with stars

GAME PLAN Draw imaginary connect-the-dot pictures with stars and create stories to go along with them.

HOW TO PLAY

This game is a more structured version of lying back, looking at the stars and thinking about the universe. Have all the players lie on their backs and find a picture in the sky: a bear, a hunter, an ice cream cone, a canoe, a goldfish, or even a school bus. Take some time to talk about the pictures everyone finds, and to point them out to each other.

Together as a group, create a story that uses all of the different pictures that your players have come up with. You can take suggestions from players and tell the story yourself, or take turns telling the story a few sentences at a time.

For example, in your story a goldfish could be taking a canoe to the ice cream shop, when a bear escaping a hunter drives a school bus off the bridge and slams into the goldfish's canoe.

VARIATIONS

To make this more of an educational game, you can have actual star charts or sample constellation pictures to show your players.

MODIFICATIONS

Players who have difficulty seeing in the dark can be in charge of the story-telling part of this game.

Lights Out

After dark is the most exciting and most nerve-wracking part of overnight camp. For seasoned veterans, it is a chance to embrace the night and play games such as Star Pictures or Flashlight Tag. For nervous novices, night time can be a scary reminder of how homesick they are. Many of our brain games and Take It Easy games can be played before bedtime to help calm excited or anxious campers.

Flashlight Tag

PLAYERS 5 or more

EQUIPMENT A flashlight

GAME PLAN Don't get caught by the flashlight; tag other players with the flashlight.

HOW TO PLAY

This game is a version of Tag played at night. (See pages 118 to 125 for other games of Tag.) To keep things safe and fun, make sure you establish boundaries and ground rules with all your campers beforehand: for instance, no going into the woods, no going past the cookhouse, no going into the cabins, no going out into the lake, etc.

Choose one player to be It. While she counts to 50 (or more) with her eyes covered at home base, the other players run and hide. It then has to find and tag the other players. The trick is, she must tag them by shining a flashlight beam on them instead of physically tagging them and calling out, "You're It!"

The first player tagged becomes the new It and everybody is called to go back to home base.

VARIATIONS

Play the game so that It must correctly call out the name of the person she has tagged with her flashlight. You can also play so that anyone who is tagged goes to "jail" and has to be rescued by another player before they can run free again.

Werewolf Tag

PLAYERS 5 or more

EQUIPMENT None, but a night with a full moon is good

GAME PLAN Don't get caught by the Werewolf.

HOW TO PLAY

Choose one player to be It. It is the Werewolf. Have the Werewolf close his eyes and count to 20 while the other players run and hide.

Then the Werewolf must try to find and tag the other players. If a player sees him, she can yell "Werewolf!" and all the other players can run to home base and be safe.

But if the Werewolf tags anyone, that player is now It and becomes the new Werewolf. Once the Werewolf has tagged someone, he has to howl out loud (like a wolf), so all the other players know there is a new Werewolf and they have to come back to home base to start a new game.

Dealing with Homesickness

The first time away from home can be both scary and exciting for campers of all ages. The first step in combating homesickness is to pump up how exciting camp will actually be. In the weeks before a child goes away to sleep-away camp, parents can talk about how exciting it is going to be, instead of how the child has to be "brave" and how much they will miss each other.

While veteran camp counselors would agree that acknowledging feelings of anxiety is important, it is also important to focus on the positive aspects of the camp experience. This means, in short, minimal time for whining.

Most camps will not allow participants to phone home unless they are seriously ill or have broken

Thorn and a Rose

PLAYERS Any number, but best with under 15

EQUIPMENT None

GAME PLAN Explore the successes and challenges of your day.

HOW TO PLAY

This game encourages players to share their feelings and encourages them to see the positive side.

Begin by asking each player to think of a "thorn" and a "rose" – something prickly and something lovely – that happened to them during the day. You might lead by example with, "I was disappointed that you guys didn't like playing cards, but I loved how much fun we had when we started playing Charades."

Participants can talk about games that they liked and didn't like, activities they found frustrating, and arguments or jokes they shared with fellow campers. This is also a great opportunity for lonely campers to receive positive reinforcement from their peers: if a participant cannot think of a "rose" that happened to them, the whole group works together to think of as many roses as possible for that one participant.

VARIATIONS

Play with the lights out and with players snuggled up in their sleeping bags or bunks.

One-Word Story

PLAYERS Any number

EQUIPMENT None

GAME PLAN Tell a story, one word at a time.

HOW TO PLAY

Have the players sit in a circle and explain that the whole group is going to create a story, one word at a time. The word energy will travel clockwise around the circle, and each player gets to say one word for each pass of the circle.

The story will begin with "Once upon a time" and end a minute or so after the leader makes a "wrap-it-up" gesture. The only big rule is that each word must make sense with the words that came before it. So, for example, if Jonah begins a story about a whale, Jasper cannot change the story to be about a camel, unless the camel is going to go to meet the whale. Encourage players to be ridiculous, but remind them that they must work with their teammates to make the story as zany as possible.

VARIATIONS

If you are playing with lights out, establish an order or way of taking turns: alphabetical or clockwise both work. For younger players, try one-sentence stories.

NOTE Make sure players keep the stories appropriate for their age and the group environment.

something. So how, then, can parents and counselors work together to combat homesickness?
- Have the campers write letters to their parents — no more than one per day.
- Play Feelings on the Floor, Thorn and a Rose, or other activities that allow participants to share their feelings.
- Find them a friend or buddy.

- Call the parents without the camper present and encourage them to send a letter explaining how proud they are of their child. (Some camps even have e-mail, and will print and hand out e-mails from home.)
- Establish a reward system or prizes for positive attitude and trying new things.

Get Them Moving

MOST OF US NEED TO WARM UP A LITTLE before any long stretch of vigorous physical activity. It's not easy to run a race from a standing start. And we need to cool down too. And sometimes we just don't want to run a race at all.

The games in this chapter require a combination of brains, reflexes, strategy and the occasional quick burst of speed. They require participants to move around but are not as exhausting nor do they take up as much space as games of tag or other Run Them Ragged games. A lot of them are good both outdoors and indoors. These are games that you can play to keep the energy up, or to transition from a low-activity part of your day, such as craft time, to a high-activity running game, and vice-versa.

The games in this section are also the most unique to a camp environment and are generally quirkier and more imaginative than the standard list of playground classics. A variety of kooky relays are included here – all of them great for building enthusiasm and friendships.

Spiderman

PLAYERS 10 or more

EQUIPMENT None

GAME PLAN To send and receive the hilarious actions of superheroes.

HOW TO PLAY

Have players stand in a circle. Before beginning the game, have players practice the sending actions and receiving actions described below.

The game begins when one player performs a sending action to another, looking them clearly in the eye so the receiving player knows that he is the recipient.

The receiving player then performs the receiving action.

Then, the receiving player performs a sending action to a new player, and the new player performs the receiving action. And so on, and so on.

All actions should be accompanied by the appropriate ridiculous noise.

- Spiderman sending action: sender slings webs and makes the sound of the webshooters as if they are Spiderman catching a bad guy.

- Spiderman receiving action: receiver must whirl around as if they are being wound up in a web and make an appropriate surprised sound.

- Wonder Woman sending action: sender shoots imaginary super bullets, making the appropriate silly shooting noises.

- Wonder Woman receiving action: receiver deflects super bullets with their shiny super bracelets.

- Alien sending action: sender mimes baby Alien crawling up and exploding out of their stomach and flying toward the face of the receiver.

- Alien receiving action: receiver grabs imaginary Alien on face and howls with agony.

- Batman sending action: sender throws Batarang and makes appropriate boomerang noises.

- Batman receiving action: receiver gets bonked on the head with the Batarang and makes bird tweeting noises as imaginary birds circle their dazed heads.

The game ends when all players have been included or when the game is peaked.

Energizers

Energizers are quick group activities that are designed to pump participants up as quickly as possible.

- Spend time the first day your group gets together learning a quick dance routine that you perform every morning. All players must dance or else they have to make up a new move.
- Have an energizing song. All participants must be singing by the time the song is over or they have to make up a new verse.
- Do a "shakedown": Have players stand in a circle and shake out their left wrist and count backwards from 10, then their right wrist backwards from 10, then their left leg from 10 and right leg from 10. Then move down from 9 shakes per limb to 1 shake per limb.

- Have a group call-back or chant.
- Have a group Clean-up Race. Divide campers into teams, set a time limit, and when you say, "Go," teams must race to clean up your camp or other location. You can deduct time penalties for messy spots or quick fixes like throwing good craft paper in the garbage instead of putting it away. To up the fun factor and difficulty level, add restrictions to your players. For example, have a three-legged clean-up race, a clean-up race to music, or a hopping clean-up race. Award points on a short-term or a long-term basis, and keep a running tally to encourage your group to keep up the good work.

Speed Rabbit

PLAYERS 6 or more, best with more than 15

EQUIPMENT None

GAME PLAN In threes, quickly form shapes and perform actions on command.

HOW TO PLAY

Have campers stand in a circle, and pick one player to go in the middle and be It.

It chooses one player in the circle to give a command to. The command will be to form one of several special positions to create a shape. If It says "Elephant!" to the player, that child and the two players immediately on either side of her must comply as quickly as possible, creating an elephant.

The last of the three players to get into position is out. The types of commands can vary from camp to camp, but here some of our favorites:

• Rabbit: The player in the middle pretends to chew a carrot, while players on either side hold their arms up in the air in bunny-ear shapes.

• Elephant: The player in the middle holds one arm straight in front of herself, looping the other arm around the first and holding her nose with her fingers. This makes the elephant trunk, which she will wave about. The players on either side must create large circles with their arms and hold them out to the side to create the ears. (See the illustration above.).

• Palm Tree: The player in the middle stands straight with arms in a V-shape. She is the palm tree. Players on either side must hula-dance, arms directed away from the palm tree.

• Elvis: The player in the middle must play guitar and knock her knees, like the King of Rock and Roll. Players on either side get on their knees and act like adoring fans.

• Television: One of the side players gets down on his hands and knees and creates a "couch" on which the middle player sits, eating a bowl of chips, and watching the third player pretend to be a television.

VARIATIONS

Speed Rabbit can be played together with Bop! (page 66).

MODIFICATIONS

In smaller groups, Speed Rabbit should be played without elimination.

PARACHUTE GAMES

The parachute is a simple piece of equipment that can produce tons of fun. Maybe it's the different colors, or maybe it's the fun waves it makes, but almost everyone loves playing with the parachute.

Parachutes generally come in two different sizes, one smaller, appropriate for 8 to 20 players, the other larger, best with 20 to 40 players. Parachutes often come with different triangles of color, which can be used to play certain games or create teams.

Sometimes, playing with a parachute can be as simple as filling it with air to make different shapes. Or have everyone sit under an air-filled parachute, the space above created by having everyone lift the parachute up over their shoulders, pulling the parachute down behind them and sitting down on the edge.

Many of the other games in the book can be modified to include the fun twist of a parachute. Two examples we mention specifically are Name Dropping (page 19) and Move Your Butt (page 20), but games such as Flying Dutchman (page 91) and even Duck, Duck, Goose (page 91) and other similar circle games can use a parachute. There are, however, some games specific to the parachute, the best of which we have included on the next few pages.

Fruit Salad

PLAYERS Best with 10 or more

EQUIPMENT Play with or without a parachute

GAME PLAN Follow the instructions to make a fruit salad.

HOW TO PLAY

Have players stand around the parachute, holding it at shoulder level, spaced evenly around the chute. Go around the circle and assign players to one of four fruit groups (for example: Banana, Strawberry, Kiwi, Grape, and then Banana, Strawberry, etc.).

Chose one player to begin in the middle, underneath the chute. Leave only enough room around the parachute for all participants (not including the one in the middle).

The game begins when the player in the middle calls one of the four fruit groups. Everyone who was assigned to that fruit group must let go of the chute and duck underneath, switching to another spot in the circle, provided the spot isn't directly on either side of him. While this is happening, the player in the middle tries to beat the other players to an empty spot around the chute.

The last person without a spot around the chute has to stand in the middle. They call out a new fruit group, and will look for a spot of their own.

Players can choose to call one or two groups of fruits at a time. So, if Ryan calls Strawberry and Grape, all the Strawberry and Grape players must switch spots around the chute.

To get things really going, a player can call out, "Fruit Salad!" Then everyone around the parachute must get up and find a new spot (but again, not a seat directly beside them). This is extra fun with the parachute slowly dropping around all the players.

VARIATIONS

For a theme day, change the names to something that fits the theme: for instance, name the groups different ice cream flavors, and call the game Banana Split.

To play this game without a parachute, just have players sit around the circle with assigned spots. When their group is called, they get up and run through the center of the circle to find another seat.

Cat and Mouse

PLAYERS 8 or more

EQUIPMENT A parachute

GAME PLAN Hide the mouse from the cat by creating bumps in the parachute.

HOW TO PLAY

Have players hold the edges of a parachute, spreading out so that the parachute is held as evenly as possible. The players should pull back until the parachute is spread out completely and participants are seated in a circle, holding the parachute down near their laps.

Choose one player to be the Mouse. The Mouse will climb under the parachute, and as long as the parachute is still, it should be fairly obvious where the Mouse is (a player-sized bump gives it away pretty quickly).

Ask participants to start pumping the parachute up and down.

This will create several ripples and bumps in the parachute, hiding the mouse.

Choose another player to be the Cat. The Cat will go on top of the parachute, searching through the fabric for the Mouse, who is allowed to move throughout the parachute.

Once the mouse is tagged, either the Cat becomes the Mouse and a new Cat must be chosen, or two new players are selected to be Cat and Mouse.

VARIATIONS

A more complex version of Cat and Mouse has the players standing, holding the parachute at shoulder height, with a small object (cheese) in the middle under the chute. The Cat begins underneath the parachute, and the Mouse begins outside the parachute.

The Cat must catch the Mouse within 20 seconds (time depending on the skill level of the participants), and the Mouse must get the cheese within the same time period.

MODIFICATIONS

For players who may have difficulty finding the Mouse on their own, use partners. That is, for the entire group (and to not single out players who find the game too challenging), have two Cats and two Mice.

Shark Attack

PLAYERS 8 or more

EQUIPMENT A parachute

GAME PLAN Be saved by a lifeguard before being eaten by a shark!

HOW TO PLAY

This game should be played on a smooth surface. Have players sit on the ground in a circle with their legs stretched out in front of them. They hold the parachute at about chest height.

Choose one player to go beneath the parachute to be the Shark. Players holding the parachute will pump it up and down to create waves that will hide the Shark.

The Shark will sneak around under the parachute and try to grab players by the leg and drag them under.

Choose one or two players to be Lifeguards. These players walk around and guard the outside of the circle.

If a player feels the tug of the Shark, he should shout "Lifeguard!" and immediately let go of the parachute. The Lifeguard will rush to his aid, and try to grab his hand before he is pulled completely under.

This part is very important – if the Shark feels a tug on the other end, she must release her hold immediately; otherwise you may have campers torn in half!

If the Shark successfully pulls the player under before the Lifeguard gets there, they may switch places, or the player also becomes a Shark. (This works only if you are playing with a particularly large group.)

NOTE Avoid playing this game with participants who are sensitive to sudden loud noises, or with nervous dispositions. This is not a game for the faint of heart!

Chute Ball

PLAYERS 8 or more

EQUIPMENT A parachute

GAME PLAN Keep a ball moving around a parachute as long as possible.

HOW TO PLAY

Have players stand, spaced evenly around the parachute, and holding it up around chest height.

Place a ball on the parachute. The goal is to have the ball continue to move around the parachute without falling into the middle hole or off the side.

Once players get the hang of it going one way, challenge them to switch directions. You can simply call out "Switch!" or say something like "Go from Stephanie to Nicole as quickly as possible."

MODIFICATIONS

Add another (different-colored) ball to raise the level of complexity, and have players send the two balls in different directions.

Color Exchange

PLAYERS 8 or more

EQUIPMENT A parachute (preferably with multiple colors)

GAME PLAN When your color is called, find another triangle with the same color!

HOW TO PLAY

Have players hold on to a color on the parachute (discourage fighting over colors). Make sure they all remember their colors.

Then, call out one of the colors in the parachute.

Everyone with that color must leave the color and run underneath the chute to another spot with the same color. For example, if Jordan and Gavin both are holding onto a blue part of the parachute, they can switch spots with each other.

If you have a large parachute, and Jordan, Gavin, Matt, Jeff and Kathi are all holding blue spots, they can switch with each other.

This can get complicated when two players try to go for the same spot at once – it can lead to scrambling last-second to find another free space.

Once you've done that a few times, you can call more than one color at once. Keep playing until everyone has had almost enough fun.

VARIATIONS

You can combine Color Exchange with Move Your Butt (page 20), and have participants swap places if they have done a particular thing. For example, in addition to calling colors to switch, you could say, "Switch places if you have brown hair."

MODIFICATIONS

If you don't have a colored parachute on hand, try playing Fruit Salad (page 78).

Parachute Golf

PLAYERS 8 or more

EQUIPMENT Two balls (different colors) small enough to fit through the center hole of a parachute

GAME PLAN Get your team's ball in the hole while keeping the other team's out.

HOW TO PLAY

Divide the group into two teams and assign each team a different color ball.

Have the group stagger themselves around the parachute (Team A player, Team B player, Team A player, etc.). They should hold the parachute waist to chest high.

Place both balls on the parachute and have players try to get their own team's ball into the hole while keeping the other team's ball out.

You can keep score for a set amount of time, or simply allow them to enjoy it.

MODIFICATIONS

To make the game more challenging, add more teams or more balls to the mix.

To make the game simpler, have teams stand all together instead of staggering them around the parachute.

Ford Angular Gear Box

PLAYERS 6 or more

EQUIPMENT None

GAME PLAN Be the fastest and the smartest cowboy.

HOW TO PLAY

All the players stand together in a circle. You might explain that in the Wild West, cowboys got tired of shooting each other all the time and often settled grudge matches with an extended battle of brains and quick reflexes, a battle they called "Ford Angular Gear Box." (Although there certainly weren't Model T Fords in the Wild West, the historical anachronism is irrelevant to the hilarity that will ensue as a result of this game.)

Have the whole group practice a Yeehaw motion: clench your fist, flex your arm and swing your fist in front of your belly. (See the illustration.) The motion isn't complete unless the players shout "Yeeehaaaaww" with their best Texas accent.

Then have the whole group practice a Hoedown motion: say "Hoedown" and pretend you are clanging the bell on an old-fashioned train (the same motion kids make to truckers to get them to honk their horns).

Then practice passing the motions around the circle. A Yeehaw swung with the right fist across the body to the left side will pass the motion to the left, and a Yeehaw swung with the left fist across the body to the right side will pass the motion to the right.

However, players cannot simply choose to change directions: players must pass exclusively to one side or the other until a Hoedown motion changes their direction. For example, if a Yeehaw passes to the right through Cherise, Jag and Simon, and Tamara makes a Hoedown motion, then the Yeehaw travels back in reverse through Simon, Jag and Cherise.

Once your group has the hang of Yeehaws and Hoedowns, introduce the Haybarn and the Gunslinger.

The Haybarn motion is made by making a roof above your head with your arms and saying "Haybarn." (See the illustration.) Haybarn causes the Yeehaw to skip a person. For example, if Cherise Yeehaw-ed Jag, and Jag made a Haybarn, the cowboy motions would skip Simon and Tamara would be next.

The Gunslinger motion is made by pointing your thumb and fingers (on both hands) like guns across the circle and, in your best Clint Eastwood voice, saying, "Gunslinger." In this case, the cowboy motion literally shoots across the circle to whomever the Gunslinger points at.

For an added level of ridiculousness, introduce the Ford Angular Gear Box. This is a whole group motion: when somebody shouts, "Ford Angular Gear Box," the whole group runs into the middle of the circle and pumps their fists downward as if they were the motor or gear box of an old-fashioned Model T Ford. The whole group shouts, "One, two, three, four," and runs back to their places in the circle.

Depending on your "house rules," the cowboy motions may either resume with the person who called Ford Angular Gear Box, or you as a leader may choose to start the motions.

You can play this game with elimination or without. Players would be eliminated if they matched the wrong word to the wrong motion, responded to a motion that wasn't passed to them, or took too long to respond.

VARIATIONS

If you like Ford Angular Gear Box, try its mystical ch'i cousin, Soh Koh No (see page 64).

However, with the added element of the whole group movement, Ford Angular Gear Box tends to be more cooperative than Soh Koh No.

MODIFICATIONS

Introduce the movements one at a time instead of two at a time.

Have the players pump their fists in place instead of running into the middle of the circle. Modify the type of movements for campers who have difficulty with large muscle coordination.

Modify the type of movements and the words that you shout to fit any theme or special event.

Kitty Wants a Corner

PLAYERS 8 or more

EQUIPMENT None

GAME PLAN Steal Kitty's corner or, if you are Kitty, find a place to lie down.

HOW TO PLAY

Have the group stand in a circle with one player (Kitty) in the middle.

Kitty approaches one of the players in the circle and says, "Kitty wants a corner, a place to lie down."

The player approached then picks somewhere else for Kitty to look, saying, "Go three people to your left," or "Go one person to my right," or whatever other arbitrary direction the player wishes to give Kitty.

The tricky part of the game comes when the other players try to annoy Kitty by switching places behind her back. For example, while Kitty is asking Vicki for a corner, Shannon and Nolan make eye contact and quickly run across the circle and switch places.

It gets even trickier when other players try to foil Shannon or Nolan! For example, if Bobby sees Shannon and Nolan make eye contact, he might slip into Nolan's spot while Shannon and Nolan are changing places. If Kitty then takes Bobby's place before Nolan gets there, Nolan becomes the new Kitty.

Peak the game when everyone is having fun.

VARIATIONS

If you like Kitty Wants a Corner, try Sword in the Stone: Supreme Master of the Universe, the more senior (and more awesome) version of this game.

MODIFICATIONS

Use hula hoops to ensure that two players don't try to slide into the same place. While we have seen this game played with chairs, we find that it can get pretty bumpy, and lessening the contact with pointy wood or metal can also help reduce injuries!

Animal Game

PLAYERS 6 or more

EQUIPMENT Pool noodle or soft foam bat

GAME PLAN Avoid being the animal caught and put in the middle of the circle.

HOW TO PLAY

Each player in the circle picks his or her own animal. No repeats! Everyone goes around the circle announcing their animals. ("My animal is a cheetah!" or "My animal is a saber tooth tiger!")

Choose one player to be It and stand in the middle of the circle with a pool noodle.

Select one player in the circle to begin the game by announcing his intention for his animal to eat another animal in the circle. (It doesn't matter if that animal would eat the other in real life or not.)

When the first player declares – for example – "Panda eats Cheetah!" then It must try to remember who was "Cheetah" and tag him with the pool noodle before "Cheetah" declares his intention to eat another animal.

If he calls out "Cheetah eats Elephant" before It can tag him, then It has to try to tag "Elephant."

If It is successful in tagging a player before he or she is able to "move up the food chain" by declaring an intention to eat another animal, It gets to switch places with that player and the game continues.

MODIFICATIONS

You may find players are left out because certain animals are repeated more frequently, and others may have been forgotten (for example, a "Komodo Dragon" might slip under the radar). To make sure these players have a chance at being It, take the opportunity to review everyone's animal names during a break in play.

SPUD

PLAYERS 4 or more

EQUIPMENT A ball

GAME PLAN Avoid getting hit four times (to spell out S-P-U-D), but try to get others to SPUD.

HOW TO PLAY

Each player is assigned a number. Play begins when one player (or the leader) tosses a ball high up in the air and yells a number.

The player whose number it is called has to run to grab the ball, while everyone else runs as far away from the ball as possible. Once the player catches the ball, he will yell, "Spud!" and everyone must freeze.

The player with the ball will then take three large steps toward the closest player, and attempt to throw the ball at that player.

If hit, the player hit gets an "S" and becomes the next person to toss the ball up. If the throw is a miss, the thrower gets an "S" and is next to toss the ball up.

The game continues until a player has a combination of four hits or misses, and has S-P-U-D. A player with SPUD is eliminated from the game.

Continue the game until it is peaked, or until all players but one are eliminated.

MODIFICATIONS

If you want the game to last longer, spell a longer word. How about SPUDNIK?

Age Groups

In some instances, we have not specifically indicated which games are appropriate for which age groups because we believe that each group of children is different. We have seen 16-year-olds and even grown adults go wild for a typically junior game such as Duck, Duck, Goose (page 91), and we have seen precocious groups of five-year-olds play typically intermediate or senior games such as Charades (page 39).

However, here are some questions to ask yourself before planning a game to make sure that it is appropriate for your group.

- What skill does your game require? Does it call for specialized skills or complicated movements?
- Does the game require strategy or higher levels of abstract thinking? For example, Giants, Wizards and Elves (page 123) requires players to have a working knowledge of Rock, Paper, Scissors, and Predator Prey (page 129) requires a basic knowledge of the animal kingdom.

- Do the children in your group have the necessary skills to succeed in your game? For example, if your game involves reading or writing, make sure participants can read or write.
- Are the children in your group able to strategize?
- What is the average level of hand-eye coordination in your group? What is the average speed?
- How well can the children in your group follow and remember instructions?
- Will the game be too easy for your group? Older players enjoy games that are still challenging. Finding ways to up the difficulty level by adding rule complications can turn a junior game into a senior game.

See the following pages for some games that are especially good for younger kids.

JUST FOR JUNIORS

Some games are good, simple introductions to the art and fun of playing games with a group. The ones we've included on the next few pages are classics most leaders will remember from their own childhood, from early school days and the first birthday parties they ever attended. These are easy enough for preschoolers to follow along and great for kindergarteners and primary grade students, but don't think that your older kids won't enjoy them — they may just put a new spin on them!

Doggy Doggy

PLAYERS At least 4, but no more than 30

EQUIPMENT Any small object such as a bean-bag or chalkboard eraser to be the Doggy's bone

GAME PLAN Steal the bone or find out who stole the bone from the Doggy.

HOW TO PLAY

Have players gather together and sit in a circle. Choose one player to be the Doggy and have her sit in the middle of the group with her eyes closed and her hands over her eyes.

Place the "bone" behind her back and tell the group that someone will have to steal the Doggy's bone. Point to one of the players so he knows he has been chosen to be the thief and must quietly sneak up behind Doggy to steal the bone. Once he has it, he has to quietly move back to his spot and hide the bone behind his back.

Then have all the children hide their hands behind their backs and lead them in chanting:

> Doggy, Doggy, who's got your bone?
> Somebody stole it from your home.
> Guess who, maybe you.
> Or maybe the monkey from the zoo.
> So wake up, Doggy, find your bone.
> If you find it, take it home!

Then the Doggy opens her eyes and tries to guess who has the bone. She has three guesses, and each time she guesses, the player she accuses has to show his or her empty hands. If she guesses correctly, the thief must show the bone and she gets to be Doggy again. If not, the player who stole the bone gets to be Doggy and play continues.

VARIATIONS

If you are playing in a classroom setting (with chairs or at desks), you can have everyone in the group sit in their seats and have the Doggy sit at the front of the room on a chair with her back turned to the rest of the group. She should not be able to see anyone in the group from where she is sitting and the bone will be placed under her chair instead of behind her.

Especially for young players, and to give everyone a chance to participate, you can choose a new thief each time and make it automatic that the player who stole the bone gets to be the next Doggy.

MODIFICATIONS

You can vary the number of guesses the Doggy has, depending on the age of your group and the number of players. The game is much more challenging when you have more than 15 participating. The fewer players you have, and the older your kids, the fewer guesses you should allow.

If you are playing with a very small group or with campers with physical challenges, try sitting very close together so that no one has to get up to steal the bone; the thief can just reach over and grab it!

Simon Says

PLAYERS 2 or more

EQUIPMENT None

GAME PLAN Follow Simon's instructions exactly; take a turn being Simon.

HOW TO PLAY

Have the group assemble and all stand facing in your direction. Then choose a leader to be Simon. For the first round, you can be Simon.

Call out an action for the players to follow, first saying the words "Simon says." For example, you say, "Simon says, stick out your tongue" and all the kids stick out their tongues. And when you say, "Simon says, pat your head and rub your tummy," all the children follow those instructions.

But when you simply say, "Touch your toes" without first saying "Simon says," whoever follows your instructions and touches their toes is out and has to sit down. The last person standing gets to be the next Simon.

MODIFICATIONS

Vary the actions and the speed at which you call out your orders according to the age and abilities of the children in your group. To make the game more challenging, players are not allowed to stop the actions they are doing until Simon says so. The faster you play, the sooner more players will be out of the game, and the sooner someone else can have a turn being Simon.

NOTE It is considered cheating if Simon asks players to do impossible things. (For example, if Simon says, "Simon says, jump up" but then follows that with "jump down," there is no way the kids can stay up, so he is asking the impossible.)

Follow the Leader

PLAYERS 2 or more

EQUIPMENT None

GAME PLAN Mimic the leader's actions; be the leader.

HOW TO PLAY

Choose a leader to be at the head of the line and have the other players line up behind her.

Then the leader must move around in different ways – jumping, bending, walking, squatting, raising an arm, pulling an ear, and so on – and all the children have to mimic her actions. Any players who do not follow the leader are out of the game. The last player still following the leader becomes the next leader.

This very simple game can also be a good game to warm everyone up and an excellent transition game. Think of it when you have to get kids to move from one place to another, as in lining up for a bus, or to do things they might otherwise not want to do, such as getting ready to go home.

VARIATIONS

To make the game a little more athletic and challenging, and if you have a large enough space, create an obstacle course to take players on, complete with running and hurdles to jump over and even stations that you set up in advance.

Catch

PLAYERS 2 or more

EQUIPMENT One or more balls

GAME PLAN Catch and throw the ball.

HOW TO PLAY

This may seem a very obvious and easy game, but a simple game of catch can often be just the right thing to get kids warmed up or cooled down or to fill time between activities. And there are many different ways to play catch, so you can adapt the game to suit the skills and number of participants.

At its simplest, you need only one ball and two players and a little bit of space around you, so you can run forward or back to catch the ball. If you are playing on a hard surface, you can incorporate a bounce in your throw. Or you can throw or catch the ball different ways (underhand, overhand, under your leg, with two hands, with your left hand, with your eyes closed, etc.).

A tennis ball is probably easiest, but you can substitute a beach ball, football, soccer ball or soft ball or even a ping pong ball. To add a bit more excitement, substitute an egg or a water balloon for the ball.

If you have more than two players, stand in a triangle, a square or a circle and pass the ball around or across the shape your group has formed.

To make the game competitive, count the number of times the ball is thrown without being dropped.

VARIATIONS

Have kids pair off and line up facing each other. Tell them to throw to their partners and each time they successfully throw and catch the ball, tell everyone to take two steps back. Pairs who miss and end up with a dropped ball must step out. The last two players still catching and throwing are the winners.

MODIFICATIONS

Add more balls of different shapes and weights to add challenge. Use balls with unpredictable bounces to make the game equally difficult for all.

Beans

PLAYERS Any number

EQUIPMENT None

GAME PLAN Be a bean.

HOW TO PLAY
Have the children follow commands and actions for each type of bean.

- Jumping bean: jump around.

- String bean: pretend to play the violin.

- Jelly bean: wobble like jelly.

- Runner bean: run around.

- Baked bean: lie on the floor with arms and legs stretched out as if sunbathing.

- French beans: do the can-can.

- Magic beans: move around pretending to wave a magic wand.

- Frozen bean: freeze.

VARIATIONS
Be creative and think up your own different kinds of beans. How about pork 'n' beans, and have kids squish up their noses and oink like pigs?

Birthday Party Plan

We imagined a seven-year-old's birthday party with about 10 kids. A high-energy event without any electronic devices!

This is a very full program and undoubtedly contains more than you can do in the average afternoon, but remember that kids who are engaged and involved are less likely to try to put your cat in the toilet or find other trouble to get into. As we mentioned earlier, it's always good to plan as many as three games for each half hour — you can't always know which ones are going to be hits and which may be flops.

Depending on the children's attention spans and the time you have allotted, pick and choose so you play as many or as few of these games as you judge will go over well.

Simply having a good list of games in mind — and prepared for in advance, if you need any equipment — can help ease any worries you might have about what the kids are going to do for all that time. So make your plans and then relax and have fun!

11:45-12:00	(as children arrive) Move Your Butt
12:00-12:30	Hot dogs, cake and presents
12:30-1:00	King's Keys; Total Recall; Cooperative Rocks
1:00-1:30	Minesweeper; Life Raft
1:30-2:00	Scavenger Hunt; snacks
2:00-2:30	SPUD; Animal Game; Red Light, Green Light
2:30-3:00	Blind Man's Bluff; Junior Charades; Dumb Crambo
3:00-3:30	Toilet Tag; Kooky Relay; Limbo Contest
3:30-4:00	Musical Chairs; Dance Freeze; Balloon Stomp (with prizes)
4:00-4:15	Going on a Picnic (as children go home)

For more about planning full days or special theme events, see pages 42 and 106.

Mother, May I?
(aka Captain, May I?)

PLAYERS Any number

EQUIPMENT None

GAME PLAN Make it to Mother by following her commands.

HOW TO PLAY

Pick one player to be the Mother. She stands at the far end of the playing field, facing away from the action. All other players are lined up on the other end, facing the Mother's back.

Players take turns asking the Mother whether they can advance a certain number of steps. For example, Patrick may ask, "Mother, may I take three steps forward?"

Mother can decide yes, no, or give him alternate directions. She may, for instance, say, "Patrick, you may not take three steps forward, but you may take two steps backwards."

To make the game even more fun, you can include Baby Steps, Giant Steps or Frog Leaps. The Mother may also decide to allow Patrick to run for a certain number of seconds, or crabwalk for a certain number of seconds.

VARIATIONS

If you've got players who aren't so keen on being asked, "Mother, May I?" because of the gender implications, you have them say, "Captain, May I?" and play with all the same rules.

Duck, Duck, Goose

PLAYERS 10 or more

EQUIPMENT None

GAME PLAN To beat It in a race around the circle.

HOW TO PLAY

This is an old favorite for a good reason: it keeps kids in a controlled space, has an element of suspense and competition, but is inclusive enough for all age groups and ability levels.

Have the group sit in a circle and choose one player to be It. If Sapna is It, she must run around outside the circle tapping all the other players on the head, in order, saying out loud with each tap the word "Duck."

The surprise comes when she says "Goose" instead of "Duck." If Sapna says "Duck, Duck, Duck, Duck" and then "Goose!" when she taps Amol on the head, Amol must jump up and run around the outside of the circle in the opposite direction to which Sapna was proceeding.

While he is running around, Sapna continues in the direction she was already headed, racing the other way around the circle to get to Amol's vacated spot.

The last person back to Amol's spot has no place to sit down and is It for the next round.

VARIATIONS

Similar games are Flying Dutchman and Larry, Curly, Moe. For a hot-weather Wet and Wild version of this game, check out Drip Drip Drop at page 146.

MODIFICATIONS

If you have children who might be a lot slower than others in running around the circle, change the way they all get around the circle to make it equally challenging for all players. For example, have them crab-walk around the circle or walk backwards or without lifting their feet.

Flying Dutchman

PLAYERS Best with 10 or more

EQUIPMENT None

GAME PLAN The lost ship the Flying Dutchman must find a port in the circle.

HOW TO PLAY

Select two players to be the Flying Dutchman. Everyone else stands in a circle, holding hands or linking arms, while the Flying Dutchman remains outside the circle, a lost ship looking for a port in the circle where it can dock.

The Flying Dutchman pair walk arm in arm around the outside of the circle, deciding on a spot.

Once they've chosen their port, they break the connection between the chosen two players by tapping their hands. They then have to race together around the circle to get back to the open port. At the same time the two players whose connection was broken have to race arm in arm around the circle in the opposite direction.

The first pair to reach the empty port rejoins the circle, and the two remaining become the Flying Dutchman and restart the search for a new port.

VARIATIONS

See Duck, Duck, Goose (left) and Larry, Curly, Moe (page 96) for similar games.

Group Sculptures

PLAYERS Any number

EQUIPMENT None

GAME PLAN Use your team's bodies to make the most interesting and beautiful sculptures, while following strict requirements.

HOW TO PLAY

Divide the group up into equal teams of three to six players.

Call out a certain combination of body parts that must be touching the floor. For example, if playing with groups of three, you might call, "Two feet, one bum, three hands and an elbow."

In this configuration, two people would stand on one leg each, with a hand or two on the floor, and one person would have her bum on the floor, with her feet raised off the floor. The "bum" person might also have her elbow or hand on the floor.

Once the team has figured out how to meet the requirements, they then must find a way to make their group sculpture interesting and beautiful.

Points are awarded for the group that finishes the fastest, and the group with the most interesting and beautiful sculpture.

VARIATIONS

Have campers try to make their sculpture look like something in particular that you choose, for example, a tree, a fountain or a piece of furniture.

Hot and Cold

PLAYERS 2 or more

EQUIPMENT Blindfold

GAME PLAN Find an object blindfolded, using hints from the group.

HOW TO PLAY

Choose one person to be blindfolded. Once that player cannot see, choose an object or location to be the desired finish point.

Then have the rest of the group guide the blindfolded player to the object using the words "Hot" and "Cold." When the player is getting closer, the group can say "Hot" and when they are moving away from the object, the group can say "Cold."

This is great in a relay form, where kids take turns to get different items to contribute to finishing a relay.

VARIATIONS

You can also split the group into teams, where each team shouts "Hot" and "Cold" at their own player. The confusion and chaos that takes over as blindfolded players try to discern their own teams' shouts can be a lot of fun!

For even more chaos, add obstacles that the blindfolded player has to avoid on the way to the object.

Horses, Knights and Cavaliers

PLAYERS Best with 12 or more

EQUIPMENT None

GAME PLAN Find your partner and perform the actions, but don't be the last pair to get in place!

HOW TO PLAY

Divide players into pairs, or have them choose a partner. One partner is A; the other is B. A partners create a circle, and B partners create a circle inside the first circle.

Have the two circles walk in opposite directions (A clockwise, B counterclockwise).

Then, call one of the following three commands, and partners must find each other and do the corresponding action.

- Horses! – One partner gets down on all fours (like a horse), while the other sits on top (like the rider).

- Knights! – One partner gets down on one knee (the knight), while the other sits on the knight's knee.

- Cavaliers! – One partner scoops the other partner up in his or her arms, as if holding a damsel in distress.

Consult the illustration to see what the action should look like.

The last pair to properly follow the action is out and can help judge or begin another game in a separate circle.

After each round, Circle A and B form up again, and you can call another command.

MODIFICATIONS

If your group has cavalier and damsel pairs not well matched for lifting, you can choose instead to have the damsel just put a leg up for Cavaliers.

Lemonade

PLAYERS 6 or more, best played with 10 and up

EQUIPMENT None

GAME PLAN Properly act out a word and avoid getting tagged.

HOW TO PLAY

Divide the group into two even teams, and send them to opposite ends of the playing area; the area should be large enough for a good, quick chase from the middle to one side.

Pick one team to go first. They must think up a profession (for instance, teacher, window-washer, doctor) and how to demonstrate it to the other team through Charades. (To learn more about the conventions of Charades, see page 39.)

The first team then approaches the other team, and a set banter occurs. It has very little to do with the game, besides the title, but nevertheless:

Team Charaders: Here we come!

Team Guessers: Where you from?

Team Charaders: (The name of their hometown.)

Team Guessers: What's your trade?

Team Charaders: Lemonade!

The Charaders must then get to work demonstrating their chosen profession to the other team. For instance, a window-washer should be fairly easy to perform.

If the other team shouts their guess and is correct, the Charaders must immediately run to their wall. If one of the Guessers tags a Charader before he reaches their home wall, the tagged player must join the other team. Then the Guessers become the Charaders.

If the other team is unable to guess, they earn no chance to gain new members, and then take their turn as Charaders.

The game ends when the players are enjoying it the most (peaking), or when one team has a significant number advantage over the other.

VARIATIONS

Similar games include Charades and Junior Charades (pages 39–40).

How to Create Even Teams

Even the most athletic child has a fear of being picked last for a team. Here are some ways to keep things fair and positive.

- Pick the teams yourself based on your knowledge of the players' skills, ensuring that the skill levels are fairly balanced and both teams have at least one positive player who can cheer on less enthusiastic teammates.
- Count off in order as A and B, or team names appropriate to the activity (for example, Manchester United vs. Chelsea for soccer, Astronauts vs. Martians for a space-themed activity).
- Instead of choosing players randomly or based on their position in the previous game, some leaders choose to make picking teams a game in itself. Ask players to sort themselves by height, and then count off. Other ways for players to sort themselves include shoe color, pant color, birthday, alphabetically and even by favorite jelly-bean color.
- Although it seems counter-intuitive to keep kids who have been fighting on the same team, occasionally being on the same team can help to develop friendships: imagine the fighting stopping if they score a goal together!
- If you insist on choosing teams the old-fashioned way, rotate the team captains so that less athletic players get their chance at choosing the teams.

Guard the Castle

(aka CN Tower)

PLAYERS 6 or more

EQUIPMENT Pylon, one or more balls

GAME PLAN Get the ball past the guard to knock down the castle.

HOW TO PLAY

Have players stand in a circle, with a pylon in the center (the castle).

Choose one player to stand by the pylon and guard it.

All other players remain in the circle, and must clasp their hands together, bending over so their clasped hands can graze the floor. Players will try to hit the ball with their clasped hands so it rolls beyond the guard and knocks down the pylon.

The guard is not allowed to stand on the pylon to prevent it from being knocked over.

The player who successfully knocks down the castle gets to be the next guard.

VARIATIONS

Name your tower and change the game to suit your theme. If your theme is World Travel, call it the CN Tower or the Eiffel Tower, or call it the Leaning Tower of Pisa, and tell everyone they have to lean to one side while hitting the ball.

MODIFICATIONS

For more people, increase the number of balls, castles and towers.

If you find the guard is "accidentally" standing on the pylon one too many times, try putting a small hula hoop around the pylon that the guard cannot step in. This also ups the difficulty level!

Jump the Creek

PLAYERS More than 2

EQUIPMENT Two pieces of string (or two yardsticks, two pool noodles, etc.)

GAME PLAN Jump over a widening creek.

HOW TO PLAY

Two pieces of string are laid parallel to each other, only a small distance apart. They should be fairly easy to jump over.

Line the players up, and one at a time, challenge them to jump the distance between the strings, or "jump the creek." They must fully clear both strings, and are allowed to take a running start.

After all players have had a turn, widen the distance between the two strings, making the creek more challenging to jump.

The game ends when only one player is able to jump the distance or when the game is peaked.

VARIATIONS

We've played this as Jump the Lava for a Hawaii theme day.

NOTE Make sure to keep the players who are out engaged in the activity (or moved on to a different activity).

Larry, Curly, Moe

PLAYERS 12 or more

EQUIPMENT Beanbags

GAME PLAN Work together in a group of three to beat the other groups of three to the center of the circle.

HOW TO PLAY

Divide the players into groups of three and pick one Larry, Curly and Moe in each group. Have all the players sit beside their partners in one large circle.

Place a pile of beanbags (numbering one fewer than the number of trios) in the center of the circle. Then have a leader call out Larry, Curly or Moe.

If Moe is called, then the two uncalled partners of each trio (each Larry and Curly duo) stand up and make a bridge with their arms while their Moe races around the circle.

When Moe gets back to his own partners he runs under their bridge, heading into the center of the circle to grab one of the beanbags. As soon as Moe rejoins his group, they all sit down.

The last group to arrive does not get a beanbag.

VARIATIONS

See Duck, Duck, Goose and Flying Dutchman (page 91).

Atom

PLAYERS 8 or more

EQUIPMENT None

GAME PLAN Create groups of numbered atoms — or else get left out in the cold.

HOW TO PLAY

Ask players to mingle with each other, walking around and making sure not to stay in one spot.

Call out a number (the maximum number is the number of participants) and the players must gather in groups of that number. If you call out "Atom Seven," for example, then the players must organize themselves in groups of seven.

Often this will leave a certain number of players out. In a cooperative version of this game, the groups must hide the odd players out in the middle of their "atom circle."

Or you can choose to play Atom with elimination, and those who end up without a group are "out." Watch out for hurt feelings, though, and consider if the cooperative version might be best for your group.

Human Ladders

PLAYERS 8 or more

EQUIPMENT None

GAME PLAN Race through the human ladders and make it back before your partner.

HOW TO PLAY

Assign each player a partner. Have the children sit in two long lines, partners facing each other, legs outstretched and feet touching. Their legs are the "ladder rungs."

Assign each pair a number and then call out one of the numbers. The pair with that number must stand up and race each other down the center of the ladder, avoiding the rungs.

Once a player reaches the bottom of the ladder, he must run around the outside of the ladder to the top and then head back down the center until he returns to his original space.

The partner who arrives at his space and sits down first earns his team a point.

The game finishes when players on one side of the ladder have earned a set number or points or when the game has peaked.

MODIFICATIONS

If you have children with poor gross motor skills, have everyone sit cross-legged to make it easier for runners to race between the lines.

NOTE Be sure to remind players not to step on the "rungs" of the ladder.

97

Evolution

PLAYERS 6 or more

EQUIPMENT None

GAME PLAN Evolve up the food chain by winning games of Rock, Paper, Scissors.

HOW TO PLAY

Begin with a large group of kids. Tell everyone that they start off as an amoeba but will have a chance to evolve. As amoebas, they wiggle around.

Have each player find a partner and play one round of Rock, Paper, Scissors. (See top right.) Whoever wins the round "evolves" into a chicken. So then the chicken must act like a chicken (with bent-elbow wings, strutting and squawking), while the amoeba wiggles around some more.

The remaining amoebas have to find other amoebas to play Rock, Paper, Scissors while the chickens try to find other chicken opponents.

The chickens who win their rounds become eagles (and eagles flap their arms as if they are flying).

When the eagles face off, the winning eagles become superhuman and flex their biceps in a body-builder pose.

But if, for instance, a chicken loses the second round, it devolves – it turns back into an amoeba. If an eagle loses, it becomes a chicken, and if superhuman loses, he becomes an eagle.

If you lose as an amoeba, you stay an amoeba.

VARIATIONS

Depending on who you ask, there are tons of variations of the steps involved. One of our favorite alternates is amoeba, snake, alligator, then T-Rex.

Rock, Paper, Scissors

This quick and classic game is good for deciding who goes first, who gets to evolve in Evolution, and simply to pass the time. Two players facing each other count out loud to three, on "one" and "two" raising one hand in a fist and then swinging it down. On "three" the players raise a hand and, as they swing it down, change the fist into one of three gestures pointed at their opponent.

A clenched fist is a rock; an open hand is paper; the index and middle figure separated and extended (like scissors) is scissors. Rock breaks scissors, so rock wins. Paper covers rock, so paper wins. Scissors cut paper, so scissors win.

Often the game is played so the best two out of three wins.

Wax Museum

PLAYERS 10 or more

EQUIPMENT None

GAME PLAN Don't let the night watchman catch the statues coming to life at night.

HOW TO PLAY

Pick one or more players to be the "night watchman," and tell the rest of the players that they are statues. Remind the group that everyone, of course, knows that at night, the statues in museums and art galleries come to life.

Give all the statues an opportunity to get into a statue-like position. When they are ready, send the night watchman to wander between the statues, trying to catch moving statues. (Breathing, sneezing, coughing and blinking are all allowed.)

When the night watchman's back is turned, the statues can sneak around and move into different positions, but they must be frozen before the night watchmen turns around.

If caught, a statue becomes another night watchman.

The game ends when only a few players (or one player) remain, or when the game is peaked.

Steal the Bacon

PLAYERS Better with 10 or more; should be an even number

EQUIPMENT One easy-to-hold item (such as a beanbag, small ball, set of keys)

GAME PLAN Be the first to steal the bacon and bring it back to your team.

HOW TO PLAY

Divide each group into two even teams, assigning each player on each team a number. For example, if you are playing with 10 participants, Team Fantastic will have players numbered 1, 2, 3, 4 and 5, and Team Amazing will have players numbered 1, 2, 3, 4 and 5.

Send each team to line up on opposite sides of a large room (or to marked boundaries outside). Place a small, easy-to-hold object such as a beanbag directly between the two teams.

Call out any of the numbers assigned and have the two players who share the number race to grab the object first and bring it back to their team's boundary or wall without being tagged by the player who shares their number who is also racing for the object.

For example, if Andrew and Janet are both assigned the number 4, when their number is called, they race to the "bacon" in the middle of the room. If Andrew is first to grab it, he must make it back to his team's starting point before Janet catches up with him and tags him.

Each time the bacon is successfully stolen, award a point to the successful team.

MODIFICATIONS

To make the game even more complex, call more than one number at a time and see if players on the same team work together or fight with each other for the "bacon." Obviously, if they're fighting over it themselves, we suggest a lesson in cooperation might be required!

MUSICAL GAMES

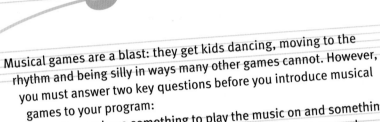

Musical games are a blast: they get kids dancing, moving to the rhythm and being silly in ways many other games cannot. However, you must answer two key questions before you introduce musical games to your program:

1. Do you have something to play the music on and something to plug your player into? Many programs aren't near ready sources of electricity or don't have stereos on site. You might need to bring your old boom box from home.

2. Do you have appropriate music? Screen your music collection to make sure it is appropriate for your age group: although songs may not contain swearing, they can still be inappropriate. Choose something that all kids can dance to and something that sends a positive, funky message to your participants.

Musical Chairs

PLAYERS 6 or more

EQUIPMENT Music and player, chairs (if chairs aren't available, see the variations)

GAME PLAN When the music stops, find a seat quickly!

HOW TO PLAY

Set up the chairs back to back, or in a circle with seats facing outward. There should be one fewer chair than players.

Start the music and have players walk around the outside of the chairs – nobody should linger next to a chair, and no touching the chairs! At random moments, stop the music. When the music is stopped, all players must scramble to find a chair.

The person without a chair is out. Take another chair away to make sure the total number of chairs is one fewer than the number of people.

The music starts again, and when it stops, another player is eliminated and another chair is taken away, and so on.

You can choose to either peak the game or have the winner be the last person sitting.

VARIATIONS

If you don't have enough chairs, use sheets of paper or hula hoops to mark the spots. Just be careful: in their hurry to drop to the floor, you may end up with some players with sore backsides!

For a more complicated, Star Wars version of musical chairs, see Star Strike (page 104).

See Musical Kickboards on page 154 for a similar game you can play in the water.

Cooperative Musical Chairs

PLAYERS 6 or more

EQUIPMENT Music and player, chairs (if chairs aren't available, see the variations)

GAME PLAN When the music stops, find a chair – even if someone else is already sitting in it!

HOW TO PLAY

As in Musical Chairs, set up the chairs back to back or in a circle with seats facing outward. There should be one fewer chair than players.

Start the music and have players walk around the outside of the chairs – no lingering next to a chair, and no touching the chairs! Stop the music at random. When the music is stopped, all players must scramble to find a chair.

Here's the twist – the person left without a chair is not out! Instead he or she must find and share a chair with someone else.

Then, take away another chair, and start (and stop) the music, leaving another player without a chair and forced to share with someone.

This continues until there is only one chair left, and the goal is to have everyone somehow "sitting" on one chair!

VARIATIONS

Another pile-on game is The Shark, on the next page.

NOTE This game involves a lot of touching and probably isn't best with players who don't want to get close to other people – by the end, everyone is somehow sitting on one another! But don't let that deter you, because it's a lot of fun.

The Shark

PLAYERS 6 or more

EQUIPMENT Several pieces of paper large enough to serve as life rafts; music and a player

GAME PLAN Find a spot on a life raft or get eaten by the shark.

HOW TO PLAY

The Shark is another version of Cooperative Musical Chairs, only without chairs! Here, instead of chairs there are large pieces of paper for each person to stand on. These are life rafts that protect them from the "sharks" that live in the ground.

Every time a piece of paper is taken away, the player left out must find a life raft to stand on to save themselves from slipping beneath the waves and being eaten by a shark!

The game ends with all players (you hope) standing on one life raft, working together to ensure no players fall off.

VARIATIONS

Once you reach the end point of The Shark and have everyone on one life raft, consider playing Life Raft (page 24), where the players must make the raft smaller, and flip it over, while still all staying on the raft.

Rikki Tikki

PLAYERS 8 or more

EQUIPMENT Music and player (for variation)

GAME PLAN Listen carefully and don't be last to touch body part to body part.

HOW TO PLAY

Divide campers into pairs and have each partner stand about 8 feet apart, facing each other. There should be two lines of partners, all facing one another.

To begin the game, shout out, "Rikki Tikki…" then two body parts together, for example: "Rikki Tikki elbow to shoulder!"

Then, the two partners must rush together and join those two body parts. For example, if Karen and Stephen are partners, Karen will take her elbow and touch it to one of Stephen's shoulders.

The last pair to complete the action is eliminated and will assist you in creating the next challenge. (One partner thinks of one body part, the other partner thinks of the second one.)

The game continues until only one pair is left, or when the game is peaked.

VARIATIONS

For a simpler game, play Body Part Match. Have the players spread out around an area. When you start the music, they should start moving around the area – walking, skipping, dancing, hopping, whatever you ask for. When you stop the music, call out a body part (for example, knee). The kids have to find one or more partners and touch knees to knees.

Vary the body part and when they get good at it, try two at a time (for instance, knees and fingers). You can play with elimination: the last pair to match body parts is out.

NOTE You will always want a leader running this activity to be the "censor" to the choices in body parts. If, for example, Neil and Peter suggest "nose to butt," you may want to encourage them to think of more appropriate body parts.

Dance Freeze

PLAYERS Best with 10 or more

EQUIPMENT Music and player

GAME PLAN When the music stops, you stop.

HOW TO PLAY

Players spread out in an open area, the music starts and everyone dances!

Tell participants they can dance in their own style to (appropriate) music. But when the music stops playing, everyone must freeze.

If you catch any players dancing after the music has stopped, they are out.

Because Dance Freeze is often played in large groups, we recommend having a second game running for players who are eliminated. If that is not possible, have the eliminated players help you watch for people breaking their "freeze."

Breathing, sneezing, coughing and blinking are definitely allowed!

Star Strike

PLAYERS 8 or more

EQUIPMENT Soft ball, hula hoops, music and player

GAME PLAN Avoid Darth Vader's "Star Strike" by touching a Rebel Base.

HOW TO PLAY

Set up fairly small boundaries with a hoop or marked circle in the middle – the boundaries should all be within throwing distance of the middle circle.

One player is chosen to be Darth Vader (It), and stands within a circle (his Death Star) holding the ball.

Hula hoops are spread throughout the room, called the Rebel Bases, each being a safe haven.

Begin playing music and have players randomly move around the area around the hoops. When the music stops, everyone except Darth Vader must not move their feet, but can reach toward a hoop to stay safe.

Those who can't reach a hoop are susceptible to Darth Vader's strike. They can dodge the ball with their upper body but must keep their feet firmly planted on the spot.

A player hit by Darth's "Star Strike" has to exchange places with him and the game continues. If Darth misses, the music starts up again and play resumes.

VARIATIONS

With more players, limit the number of players who can touch a hoop to be "safe."

In a very large group, have those hit become Stormtroopers. They stay in the spot they were hit, and Darth Vader can toss the ball to them if they have a better shot at getting another player out. There is still only one attempt to get another player out per round.

Tunes on a Topic

PLAYERS Any number

EQUIPMENT Pencil and paper

GAME PLAN Out-sing the opposing team with song lyrics about a particular theme or topic.

HOW TO PLAY

This game works best with preteens and teenagers who listen to music. Divide the group into two teams and give each team a pencil and piece of paper. Announce the "topic" – love, summer, trees, rain, rock and roll, school or cars, for example. Have each team write down as many songs as possible that incorporate the target topic within a one- or two-minute time period, then ask them to put their pencils down.

Choose one team to start and have them sing the lyric that incorporates that theme. For example, if the theme is love, potential lyrics could include "All you need is love" (The Beatles, complete with "bah da dah da dah" for the trumpets), and "Got me looking so crazy in love" (Beyoncé Knowles).

Teams alternate singing lines back and forth to each other but cannot repeat the same song. The group with the most songs left when the game is peaked wins.

Limbo Contest

PLAYERS 3 or more

EQUIPMENT Music and player; a long stick

GAME PLAN Find out how low you can go ... and then try to go lower!

HOW TO PLAY

Have two players or leaders hold either end of a stick horizontally at about the average shoulder height of the participants. Players line up behind the stick and, one at a time, lean backwards and dance under the limbo stick. If they fall, touch the ground with any-thing other than their feet, or touch the stick, they're considered out.

After all participants have had an opportunity to try the stick at that height, lower the limbo stick and everyone who made it the first time gets to go again. The stick is lowered by a little after each round. The winner is the player still able to pass under the stick when no other player can make it under without touching the limbo stick or falling.

Limbo is often played in large groups, and so we recommend having a second game running for players who are eliminated, so they don't have to just be observers.

MODIFICATIONS

If you have players who are really young or not steady on their feet, you can let them crabwalk under.

To make the game more challenging, play it on ice or on roller skates.

THEME DAYS

At our favorite camps, at least once a week, our counselors dressed up in wacky costumes and sent us on an adventure. A theme day is when all the leaders — and sometimes even the kids — dress up in one particular theme of costume: under the sea, space, cowboys, robots, Olympic athletes, mad scientists, Robin Hood, Medieval Times, Ancient Egypt and Superheros are all great examples, as are trendy movies, books or TV shows.

The leaders work together to create a story-line, such as "an evil mad scientist has come to take over camp, and all the kids have to work together to defeat him through learning about science." One of the leaders would dress up as the evil scientist, and the other ones would dress up as the good scientists. The leaders then take the kids through a series of games and events to "train them" as scientists. They can collect clues and ingredients to an experiment (baking soda and vinegar, or borax and white glue) by completing the events.

All of the games and activities should be modified to fit the theme day, simply by changing the title and a few rules. A game of dodgeball can be called "Avoid Atomic Chaos." The day is over when the kids follow the clues to construct the experiment and defeat the evil scientist. You can then award them science diplomas, or give them a piece of atomic goo to take home with them.

Having a theme day is a great way to end a week. You can get the whole camp involved by having different groups compete for the clues. Theme days are also great opportunities to build friendships between older and younger campers, as you can split the camp up without dividing into age groups and have the older campers be "team captains."

Crazy Costumes

While we had an extensive costume box at our home growing up, we never spent more than ten dollars on our camp costumes. Instead, we taped craft supplies to our hats and used objects we found around the house: tin foil, pipe-cleaners, stuffed animals, and yellow rain pants served us for our robot, mad science, animal safari and firefighter costumes, respectively.

That being said, when designing your costume, remember that you must be able to move, take care of the kids, and run in case of emergencies, so costumes that are one giant box with high heels are a no-go. Make sure your costume is also heat resistant: there is nothing that spoils the mood faster than a Superhero who removes his sweaty spandex jumpsuit to reveal the boring old camp uniform underneath.

Modifying Games for Themes

An exciting way to change up your everyday recreational or school program is by having a theme day. Leaders can dress up as special characters and engage with younger children in make-believe, or engage older children in a special competition.

You can change almost any game in this book just by changing the name and by twisting a few rules. For example:

• For a Rock Star Makeover theme, play Slow-Motion "Catwalk" Tag, (page 120) using fashion runway moves and air guitar.
• For an Under the Sea theme, change Ship to Shore (page 114) to Sea to Shore and include types of fish, whales, mermaids, and surfer dudes and dudettes as possible actions.
• For an Army theme day, dress as a drill sergeant and develop a kooky relay (page 108) based on the standard basic training obstacle course, and follow that up with a game of Minesweeper (page 32).

Zany Food

Everyone likes playing with food — it can be gross and yummy. Although programs today have to be aware of allergies and often are required to get permission from parents before feeding campers anything, these food-based activities are some of our favorite camp games. Make sure you have gung-ho leaders and participants with strong stomachs before attempting these activities.

MARSHMALLOW STRUCTURES Using large marshmallows and straws, or small marshmallows and toothpicks, race to build structures. Award points for height, stability, and architectural beauty. If the structures were built with clean hands on clean surfaces, the winners can eat the marshmallows, but this is also a great way to use up stale marshmallows from the beginning of the summer.

MARSHMALLOW SONGS Have participants see how many marshmallows they can stuff in their mouth, while still being able to sing the national anthem or other camp song.

JUST LIKE MOM This event is a great wrap-up to a week-long challenge between members of a group or between different groups. This activity also works at the end of a theme day, as you can have themed "menus." Throughout the session, award food ingredients as prizes. At the end of the week, divide participants into groups, making sure that each group gets a variety of ingredients. All of the ingredients should require no refrigeration, be nonperishable (no dairy) and allergy-free: ketchup, fruit punch, dried cereal, gummy worms, hot sauce, rice cakes, cookies and canned beans are all good examples.

Give campers anywhere between 20 to 30 minutes to combine their ingredients and make a marvelous meal for the leaders or program directors. The leaders must then taste each of the camper's concoctions, no matter how vile. Watching the leaders' facial expressions is the highlight of this game. We have three awards: taste, presentation and yuck-factor, so that even groups with terrible ingredients (a hot sauce-gummy worm-cereal combo) can earn points.

FOOD FACIALS As with Just Like Mom, award ingredients as prizes throughout the day or week: canned whipped cream, cucumber and olive oil are safe bets, but for variety consider orange concentrate, apples, apple sauce and peanut butter (after an allergy check). Allow campers to whip up their materials and give the leader a "makeover" with the food ingredients. For added hilarity, have leaders do a runway walk with their face covered in applesauce and peanut butter.

DIGGING FOR WORMS Hide a few gummy worms or gummy bears in paper plates full of either whipped cream or dried cereal. Place the plates either down on the ground or on a table. Choose a few competitors and have them stand, sit or kneel behind the plates with their hands behind their backs. Players must dig through the whipped cream with their mouths, suck up the gummy worms and spit them out. The first player to find all their worms wins. For added difficulty, blindfold the participants.

- For a Witches and Wizards theme day, obviously play Giants, Wizards, Elves (page 123), but follow that up with a twist on standard Charades, where instead of guessing random phrases, team must guess types of spells — invisibility, immunity, levitation or truth-telling, for example.
- For a Mad Science theme day, play Mother, May I? (page 90), but substitute names of famous inventions. For example, "Mother, may I invent the atomic bomb?" "No, take four steps backwards." "Mother, may I invent a cure for cancer?" "Yes, take 10 steps forward."
- For a Superhero theme day, play Predator Prey (page 129) with the names of superheros and supervillains instead of predators and prey, followed by a game of Spiderman (page 76), and perhaps Evolution (page 98), and finished off with a game of Octopus, modified so that all players have to walk like penguins, with the Octopus playing the role of Batman catching the Penguin.

RELAY RACES

For the following races, you'll need to have a basic understanding of how a relay race works. Begin by dividing your campers into even teams. If you have odd numbers, some teams may need to have a player run the race twice. Choose one person from each team to start the race.

Set up a start line and have the starting player from each team sit behind the line with space between them. Have the rest of the team line up behind the starting player, sitting down. (You can have your players remain standing, but we find sitting makes crowd control easier.)

When you say "go," the first runner from each team moves through the course. When he is finished the course, he tags the second runner, who then moves through the course.

You have two options for setting up your relay course. You can set your course up in a rectangular space and have the start line at one end and the turn-around point at the other end. With this shape, the running player tags the person at the front of the line. Or, you can set your course up as an oval or circle and have the running player sit down at the back of the line to get the second runner going. The disadvantage to this layout is that the team on the inside track will have the advantage, but a circular layout often works best for relay races based on natural geographic features — an obstacle course around a lake, for example.

Depending on the number of leaders you have available, it is often a good idea to have one leader at each "station" of the race to ensure that participants are not cheating by doing one spin of a hula hoop instead of five. This also allows for leaders to help participants cheat — if a camper cannot hula hoop to save her life, the leader can allow her to move forward after she has made five attempts.

Over-Under Relay

Have players stand one behind the other.

The first player holds a small-to-medium-sized ball, and passes it over her head to the player behind her. The second player takes the ball and passes it under his legs to the third player, who then takes it and passes it over her head to the fourth player, who – you guessed it – passes it under his legs to the fifth player.

This continues until it reaches the last player. The relay can end here, or the last player can run to the start of the line and begin the pattern again until all players have been at the front of the line.

The team's goal can be to beat their own best time or to beat another team. If playing against a team larger or smaller, have the smaller team repeat players to even up the number.

Tunnel Relay

This relay should take place on a smooth surface, and time should be allowed for lots of mistakes!

Have players lined up, standing one behind the other, with their legs spread apart, allowing enough space for a ball to roll underneath. When everyone is in position, you or the first player can aim and roll the ball under everyone's legs.

The relay is successful if the ball goes under every player's legs. You can repeat it by having the final player catch the ball and run to the front and repeat it.

Make the relay more difficult by spacing the players further apart.

For cooling hot-weather relays, see the Firefighter Relay and Wet T-Shirt Relay at page 147 in Wet and Wild.

Blind Artist/Blind Writer

Have players sit cross-legged in a line, all facing the back of the person in front of them (except the first player, who is seated at the front with a piece of paper and pencil).

Using your finger, draw a simple pictogram or short word on the back of the last player in line. The last player then must try to recreate the pictogram or word on the back of the player in front of him.

For example, if you draw a simple flower, or trace the word "CAT" on Filipe's back, he should try to do the same to Valerie in front of him. Then Valerie will try to do the same to the player in front of her, and so on, so the word or symbol proceeds all the way to the front of the line.

Once the first player in line has "received" the message, she will try to recreate it on the piece of paper, trying to get it as close to the original picture or message as possible.

How to Create a Kooky Relay

Relays always seem like an extra-special event, and can encourage friendships between group members. However, camp relays should have some special element beyond the basic there-and-back running around a track passing a baton.

To begin, gather up any equipment you have on hand and take a look at it. You must have enough of each item (for example, baseball bats) for each team. Some items are easily substitutable (for example, hockey sticks can substitute for baseball bats; backpacks can substitute for pylons).

Divide up your teams evenly. If a team has one fewer person, they should pick a team member to go twice. Although teams should be encouraged to cheer their players on, a good way to keep the kids organized is by having them stand in a line and then sit down when they have completed their turn. A team has to be all sitting down to win!

The best relays are ones that contain several stages and act both as an obstacle course and relay race. Suggested stages include, but are by no means limited to:

- "tightrope walk" along a skipping rope or chalk line
- hula hoops to pass through or jump over (army basic-training style)
- hula hoops to spin around your middle for a set number of times (for example, 3, 5, 10)
- holding on to a baseball bat, place your forehead on one end and bend over so that the other end is on the ground. Spin your body around, keeping your forehead on the baseball bat, for a set number of times.
- dribble a ball (basketball, soccer) through a series of pylons
- toss a beanbag at a target
- take a set number of turns with a jump rope
- blow a ping pong ball across a line
- move a tennis ball with your nose across a line
- carry water balloons (especially good on a hot day), an egg on a spoon, a ball in a scoop, or Cheerios on a toothpick

Balloon Pass

Have players line up. Give the first player a balloon to hold between his legs. Tell him to try to pass it to the next player without using his hands.

The balloon must be passed all the way down the line from knees to knees without it hitting the floor. If it falls, the relay must start over.

A similar game is the Beach Toy Relay on the next page.

Ice Floe Race

For this race, best played on a smooth playing surface, you will need some big sheets of paper: regular newspaper works well.

Divide players into small groups of three or four players. Tell them that they have to race across the Arctic Ocean on the ice floes without falling into the water.

Give each team two pieces of newspaper and have them line up at the starting line. When you say Go! each team will have to put down one piece of paper, then all of the team members step on that one piece of paper. Then they put the second paper down, everyone steps on it; they pick up the first paper, put it down, everyone steps on it, and so on until they are at the finish line, across the ocean.

If any player falls off the ice floe and touches water, the whole team has to go back to the beginning and start again. The first team to successfully cross the ocean wins.

Play this as a relay race by having players take turns crossing the ocean separately. The first team to have all players successfully across wins.

Orange Pass

Have players line up. Give the first player an orange. She has to tuck the orange between her chin and shoulder, and pass it to the same spot between the chin and shoulder on the second player.

As with the balloon pass, if the orange falls on the floor, the relay starts over.

Leapfrog Relay

Divide kids into two or more teams and have each team line up one player behind the other at the starting line.

The first player on each team should be ready, squatting low, head down and palms on the ground. When you give the signal "Ready, set, go!" the second player, already standing behind the first player, places his hands on her back and, keeping his feet out to the sides, pushes off and jumps over her.

The second player should then get down low for the third player to jump over, and so on, until everybody has leapfrogged and you get to the end of the line. Players keep leapfrogging to the finish line. Declare in advance how the winner will be decided: the first team to reach the finish line or the first team to get every player on the team across the finish line.

Group Challenges

Many relays can also be used as group challenges. In the case where you have several groups (as in a camp environment), activities such as the Over-Under Race, Blind Artist and all of our other Kooky Relays can be used to generate healthy (and we emphasize healthy) competition between the groups and encourage team-building within the group. Use group challenges to award points, break a tie or even to determine which group gets to go for lunch first.

Beach Toy Relay

You need one Frisbee or plastic plate plus one mid-sized inflatable beach toy or other soft, light object for each team. We actually first played this game at a women's adventure boot camp with an inflatable dolphin and shark. Our two teams were the Dolphins and the Sharks!

Divide players into two or more teams and set up your relay course, establishing a start and finish line and a turnaround point. Have teams line up behind the first player on each team.

Give the first person on each team his or her toy and tell them to hold the toy between their legs (knees are okay but thighs work better). Then give them each a Frisbee to hold above their head with both hands. Then, when you say "Go!" players must race to the turnaround point and back without dropping the toy. If the toy is dropped, players can pick it up and put it back between their legs, but they cannot hold on to it while running.

The tricky part comes next, when the players must transfer their toys from between their legs to between the legs of the next player on the team without either of them using their hands.

The first team with all players to the turnaround point and back wins.

Beanbag Balance Race

You will need one beanbag for each team to play this game.

Divide players into two or more teams and establish a starting line and turnaround point. The route between the two points doesn't have to be straight but make sure there are no objects in the way such as tree roots or rocks that might be tripped over.

Have the first person in line on each team place a beanbag on top of his or her head. When you say, "Go," players race to the turnaround point and back, keeping the beanbags balanced on their heads. If a beanbag falls, the player must pick it up and continue where he or she left off back to the finish line to hand to drop the beanbag on the ground for the next player to put on top and balance. The first team with all players there and back wins.

Ways to Make a Relay More Difficult

- Have players crawl, crab-walk, slither, bunny hop, hop on one foot, cartwheel or walk backward through stages.
- Have players place an orange or tennis ball between their knees.
- Have players wear a floppy hat.
- Have players act like an animal or famous person at different points in the relay (for example, when carrying the an egg on the a spoon, participants must advance forward like old-fashioned sword-fighters).

Run Them Ragged

THERE ARE TIMES in every camp counselor, program leader, teacher and parent's week when they wish they could just send the children in their charge around a track and make them run laps until they are too exhausted to misbehave.

While this may seem cruel and unusual punishment, it does have a basis in reality: kids who use up their energy have less energy to misbehave. However, while energetic kids might misbehave when they are bored, exhausted kids just get cranky and miserable. So, with that grain of salt, play the games in this section as part of a balanced day, and allow for recovery time and water breaks during and after the game.

These games generally require large spaces and a fair bit of running: enough to raise the heart rates of all of the participants. Although many of the games can be played indoors, in spaces such as gyms, they are the most fun outdoors. We've included a slew of classic and amusing variations of Tag in this chapter. There's bound to be one that is new to you.

Although most of these games are not based on any one specialized sports skill, because of the relatively high level of cardio exercise, they tend to favor the athletes in the group. However, the games in this section are probably our favorites: they are fast-paced, exciting and sometimes quite competitive. They leave us just a little bit breathless, but always with big smiles on our faces.

Ship to Shore

PLAYERS Any number

EQUIPMENT None

GAME PLAN Be the fastest sailor at camp, quickly obeying the commands of the leader — no matter how silly.

HOW TO PLAY

Shout out various "commands" that the players must quickly obey. The commands tend to be nautically themed. Some actions are sillier than others. Favorites include:

- "Starboard" – players must run to the right-hand side of the playing area,

- "Port" – they run to the left,

- "Bow" – they run to the front end of the playing area,

- "Stern" – they run to the back end,

- "Scrub the Decks" – players must get on their hands and knees and mime scrubbing,

- "Captain's Coming" – they stand straight at attention, hand ready to salute,

- "Climb the Rigging" – they mime a climbing motion,

- "Submarine" – players lie down on their backs with one leg straight up in the air (as the periscope),

- "Captain's Daughter" – they twirl their (invisible) hair and bat their eyelashes,

- "Sharks" – players scream as loudly as possible, but use your discretion in calling this one.

For maximum silliness, call out two commands at once and enjoy the actions.

You can play the game with elimination, so the last player to perform each activity is out, or simply peak the game.

VARIATIONS

You can also play this game so that the leader also alternates as It when the command "Fish Gobbler" is called out. Players must quickly drop to the floor and find one another and attach arms, legs or bodies before being tagged. Players are safe as long as they are physically linked together.

If you are playing elimination, players tagged before linking up are eliminated from the game. Regular play is resumed by calling "Rescue!"

MODIFICATIONS

Instead of using complicated nautical terms, play Here, There, Where. This game involves the same kind of actions as Ship to Shore but is simpler.

When you call "Here," children run to you. For "There," point in a direction and the kids run there. For "Where," kids stop and jump up and down.

Dragon Tails

PLAYERS 12 or more

EQUIPMENT Pinnies or flags

GAME PLAN Steal the other dragons' tails.

HOW TO PLAY

Divide the group into even teams with three or four players per team. Appoint one person to be the dragon's head and one person to be the dragon's tail. The other team members are the dragon's body.

Give the player who is the dragon's tail the pinnie or flag so that he can tuck an end of it into his pants. Most of the "tail" should be hanging out and it should come out easily when tugged at.

After setting boundaries, position the teams far apart from each other. Have the teams form dragons by placing their hands on the shoulders of the person in front of them. The dragon's head should be at the front of the line, and the dragon's tail should be at the end.

Dragons must move as a unit and attempt to steal the other dragons' tails. Only the head of the dragon can grab at the other tails.

Once the tail of a dragon is stolen, that dragon unit is out. If a dragon unit breaks apart, they are "out."

If playing with elimination, the winning dragon is the last team standing.

VARIATIONS

To play without elimination, have "out" teams count to 30, or some other number, before rejoining the game.

Pros and Cons of Elimination Games

Elimination games are great for increasing competition between campers and groups of campers. For older participants, or participants who are "too cool for camp," the incentive of possibly being declared "winner" is enough to get them to play the game in the first place. There is, however, a difference between competitive games, which teach players to work as a team, and elimination games, which end in a "last person standing" showdown.

Elimination games work well with highly competitive and equally skilled groups of participants, or with participants who have a variety of different types of skills (so that the kid with the quick physical reflexes wins one time and the kid with the superior brain-puzzling skills wins another time). Elimination games also work well if you "peak" them before there is only one player left — that way, you get five champions instead of one.

However, once kids are eliminated, that means they are out of the game and can get bored and into trouble when not engaged and not as closely supervised.

Elimination games do not work well early on in your program's session while participants are still getting to know each other, nor are they as successful with particularly sensitive groups of children. Finally, when working with campers with special needs, use elimination games sparingly so that those campers don't spend a lot of time on the sidelines, or modify all or part of the game so that those campers can achieve success. For more ideas on inclusion and modifying games, see Modifying Games for Abilities (page 26) and Inclusion Is for Everyone (page 27).

For games in which everybody wins, look for this icon. 🏆

115

Red Light, Green Light

PLAYERS 3 or more

EQUIPMENT None

GAME PLAN Get to the opposite side without being caught by the traffic cop for driving through a red light.

HOW TO PLAY

Establish clear boundaries, particularly a starting point and end point.

One player (the traffic cop) stands at the end point, back facing the other players lined up at the starting point. You can start the game as the cop or choose one of the players.

The traffic cop can call out, "Red Light, "Green Light," or "Yellow Light."

Players must freeze during "Red Light," are allowed to move as quickly as they can during "Green Light," and must move in slow motion during "Yellow Light."

When the traffic cop calls "Red Light," he will immediately turn around and try to catch his fellow players still in motion.

Players who are caught have to return to the starting point. The first player to reach the end point is the new traffic cop.

Chuck the Chicken

PLAYERS 6 or more

EQUIPMENT Any throwable object such as a beanbag, to serve as the chicken

GAME PLAN Try to throw far and be the fastest team and run around the group the most times.

HOW TO PLAY

Divide the players into two teams. One team yells, "Chuck the chicken," and throws the object as far as they can.

While the other team is running to retrieve it, the chucking team bunches together in a group and one member of the chucking team runs around the group as many times as she can before the other team gets the chicken, with teammates counting out loud the number of times she goes around.

The opposing team member who gets the chicken chucks it again and then the teams switch, so the other team is now dashing after the chicken, while the team that threw the chicken is bunched up with one member running around their group.

This is a good transition game, to play while waiting for another event or activity, as there is no real end to the game.

VARIATIONS

"Kick the Chicken," a close cousin to Chuck the Chicken, can also double as a modification on Soccer Baseball if you don't have a baseball field.

Here, the Chicken should be a ball or other kickable object. One team "kicks the chicken" as far away as they can. Another difference is, the number of times the group representative circles the kicking group equals "runs," as in baseball.

As with Chuck the Chicken, when the other team gets the ball and kicks it, the team must stop counting runs and go after the Chicken, while the other team chooses a representative to circle them, counting the number of runs earned.

The game is played until a number is met (for example, first team to score 15 runs) or to a set time.

Crab Soccer

PLAYERS 6 or more

EQUIPMENT Ball, net markers

GAME PLAN Score a goal on your opponent's net.

HOW TO PLAY

Play this game with the same rules as soccer, except campers must play with their hands and feet on the ground, torso facing up. In this way, they are scurrying like crabs across the playing field rather than running.

It is advisable to decrease the size of the playing field, since it will take much longer for players to move.

Frolf

PLAYERS Any number

EQUIPMENT Frisbee(s) and target markers (for example sticks, small flags or natural markers such as trees)

GAME PLAN Try to get to the target in as few Frisbee throws as possible.

HOW TO PLAY

Frolf is a combination of Frisbee and golf. Players must toss a Frisbee toward a marker, trying to hit or have the Frisbee land on the marker in as few throws from the starting point as possible.

You will have to set up your course ahead of time, but there is no set distance between "holes" and the course can have any number of targets.

If there are a lot of players and not enough Frisbees, players can create teams and play Frolf Scramble, taking turns throwing the Frisbee. For example, Fraser throws the initial "drive," Robbie throws it onto the "green" and Cam throws the short and precise "putt" required to hit the marker.

Count one point for each throw. The player or team with the lowest score wins.

TAG! YOU'RE IT!

At its most basic, a game of Tag begins when someone touches a playmate and shouts, "Tag, you're It!" If Peter tags Maureen, then Maureen becomes It and she has to run around and chase the other players till she tags someone, and then that someone becomes It. And so it continues until everybody is worn out, it is time to go home or the street lights come on.

For an organized game of Tag, choose one player to be It. It has to stand at home base (a tree, a big rock, a corner of a wall or some other fixed location) and cover her eyes and count to 50 (or 25 or 100) while the other players run. Then It goes out to try to find and tag the other players. Any player who can sneak by It and get to home base without being tagged is safe. The way we play it, when a player is tagged, It shouts out, "Tag! You're It" and that person becomes the new It and has to go back to home and start counting again. You may know other variations of the game.

Tagging, it should be mentioned, is not hitting: a gentle tap on the shoulder is perfectly appropriate, but a sock in the stomach is not.

Ways to Choose It

- Counting off with eeny meeny miny moe or other silly rhymes
- the person who won the last game is It
- the person who won the last game chooses It
- choose the person who listened the whole time you explained the rules
- choose someone sitting/standing nicely and quietly with their hand raised
- choose the person who can scream the loudest
- choose the person with the best dance move
- choose the person with the best giraffe (bunny, lizard, etc.) face
- choose the person who answers the trivia question correctly

Rhymes for Choosing It

Eeny meeny miny moe,
Catch a tiger by the toe,
If he hollers let him go,
Eeny meeny miny moe.

Ink stink
Bottle of ink
Someone let out
An awful stink
It was Y-O-U!

Baby, baby, suck your thumb
Wash it off with bubble gum.

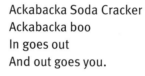

Ackabacka Soda Cracker
Ackabacka boo
In goes out
And out goes you.

My momma and your momma
Hanging out the clothes
My momma punched your momma
Right on the nose.
What color was the blood?
R-E-D spells red and you are it!

Each, peach, pear, plum
Out goes Tom Thumb,
Tom Thumb won't do,
Out goes Betty Blue,
Betty Blue won't do,
So out goes you.

Not because you're dirty
Not because you're clean
Just because you kissed a boy (girl)
Behind a magazine.

Engine engine number nine
Rolling down the Chicago Line
If the train jumps off the track
Do you want your money back?
Yes, no, maybe, so,
But Y-O-U are It!

Pairs Tag

Divide the group into teams of two (or have players choose one partner). One partner is Player A and the other partner is Player B. Player A is It, and Player B is being chased. Have them start the game a fair distance away (opposite sides of the boundaries). Once Player B is tagged, she must twirl around three times (to prevent endless tagging back-and-forth between players), and then take chase after Player A. Pairs tag must be peaked to end the game.

Beanbag Tag

Except for one or more Its, each player must place a beanbag on his or her own head. Players are only safe from It as long as the beanbag remains balanced. Players are not allowed to hold the beanbag in place. If the beanbag falls off, the player becomes frozen and can be tagged by It. When tagged, a player becomes another It.

Other players must try to prevent It from gaining more players to their side by placing the fallen beanbag on the frozen player's head before they are tagged by It.

Make it simpler for younger players by having no It; players just work together to stay unfrozen.

Make the game more complex by shouting out speeds the players have to follow. Or play at "super fast" speed; balancing a beanbag on your head while moving quickly can be quite challenging for even the most adept player.

Manhunt

Begin the same way as conventional tag. When It tags a player, that player also becomes It. Each time a player is tagged, the It team grows and the escaping team shrinks. The game ends when all the Its go on a Manhunt to catch the last player. The last player tagged becomes the first It in the next round.

Blob Tag

Begin in the same way as conventional tag but within smaller boundaries. Choose one It to run around trying to tag other players.

However, when It tags a player, that player joins It by holding hands or linking elbows and also becomes It. This continues, with more players getting tagged and being added on to the Blob of It.

The Blob works together to catch the rest of the players, but it must stay together to retain its power; if the Blob is broken, it cannot tag players.

Eventually, the entire group save one or two members will be part of the Blob, and the game can end then, or after the Blob has cornered and caught all remaining members. This game works best in a playing field with distinct lines, perhaps even one with walls, so that players can be cornered by the Blob.

PacTag

This game is best played on a gymnasium floor with lines, but lines can be created almost anywhere using sidewalk chalk or masking tape.

The game begins with one or more Its, who will try to catch the other participants. However, both It and the other players are only allowed to walk on the lines on the floor (a bit like in the video game PacMan, where you have to stay within the lines).

Once tagged, you also become an It. The game ends when only one player is left to be tagged.

This game is best played with a "walking only" rule, because running will likely lead to sloppy following of the lines-only rule. If you're playing this game on a grassy surface, instruct players to walk in straight lines and only turn on right (90 degree) angles, as if they were walking around several squares.

Slow Motion Tag

Slow motion tag follows the same premise as high-speed tag, only instead of everyone running, everyone moves in slow motion. It takes a disciplined group of players to have a good game of Slow Motion Tag, but the hilarity is well worth the discipline.

Contain players to a space no larger than an average classroom. Appoint two or three people to be It and give them an item such as a pencil, marker, ruler or flag to signify that they are It.

Demonstrate the speed level that you expect from your players. We recommend playing at about a quarter of normal speed. Using the metaphor of moving through peanut butter often helps children understand. Also explain that because gravity does not work in slow motion, one foot must stay on the ground at all times – so no jumping out of the way.

The game begins with all of the Its on one side of the space and all of the runners on the other. It goes after the runners in super slow motion. The runners can pivot, dodge and twist out of the way, but must do so in slow motion. If It tags a runner, It passes along their signifiers (pencils, flags) to the person tagged. We do this so it is easy to tell who is It, which is important in a game that focuses more on observation than reaction time.

After a few initial "role-modeling" rounds, we recommend that this is the one game that you do not play alongside your campers. It is important here to have an outside observer encouraging participants to keep the pace slow. The plus side of all this slowing down is a game of tag that ends up looking like a kung-fu ballet in super slow motion.

Encourage players to pretend they are moving like the characters in a movie shown in slow motion and you will get groovy results.

Category Tag

Pick a category before playing the game – for example, Television, Fruit or Sports.

If Noel is It, he will try to tag other players before they are able to squat and name something from that category. For example, when playing Fruit Tag, to avoid being tagged, John could squat and shout out, "Strawberries!" or "Apples!"

Players must call out something from that category before being tagged. Noel must leave players alone if they have successfully called out something from that category.

Often players will crack under pressure, squat and be unable to think up anything.

If John is tagged, he becomes It.

This game can be made academically challenging by having the category relate to a school subject – for example, the category could be multiples of seven or names of countries.

For Tag games to play in the dark, see Flashlight Tag and Werewolf Tag at page 72.

FROZEN TAG (aka Freeze Tag)

In Frozen Tag, also known as Freeze Tag, there are one or more Its who chase the other players. If It tags a player, the player becomes frozen and has to rely on another player to unfreeze them and get them back into the game. In basic Frozen Tag, players are unfrozen by having another player crawl between their legs.

There are tons of variations with different themes and different ways of unfreezing to match the themes, resulting in some of our favorite games of all time.

We like Frozen Tag as an alternative to regular tag because the game is constantly moving and players all have to work together to help each other stay in the game. This encourages a great rapport among players — the "cool kid" may have to rely on the "shy kid" to get back into the game. Since Frozen Tag is often fast-paced, players don't stop to think about who they are or are not unfreezing. It's a great clique-breaking game, and lots of fun too.

Make sure to take the opportunity to switch up It.

Lightning Tag

It is Zeus, ruler of the Greek gods, and god of sky and thunder. Zeus tags players by throwing his lightning bolt (a pool noodle or soft ball serves as a reasonable alternative to real lightning). The tagged player remains frozen until another player comes and spins them, bringing them back into the game.

Toilet Tag

If tagged, players squat down with one arm stretched out. Another player must come and press down on the outstretched arm, essentially "flushing" the toilet, before the frozen player can return to the game.

Cow-Tipping Tag

Based on the mythical activities of rural hooligans, this game is one of our favorites. The farmer is It. Once tagged, a player must go on her hands and knees and moo like a cow. She remains a cow until another player comes and tips her over to unfreeze her.

Hot-Dog Tag

When tagged, players must lie flat on the ground, arms at their sides, much like a wiener. To unfreeze, two other players must come and lie on either side of the frozen player, acting as the bun.

This game can be made trickier by adding condiments – for example, a player holding a red ball (ketchup) would have to come touch the hot dog and buns before they can unfreeze. If a red ball isn't handy, yellow (mustard), green (relish) or any other colors will do.

Setting Boundaries

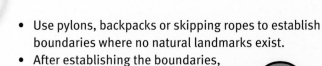

Setting boundaries is an important step in any game, particularly active games. Here are some suggestions:

- Consider the speed of your players and how far they can run without exhausting themselves.
- Consider your ability to supervise the whole playing field, and manage any safety hazards.
- Use natural and built landmarks such as trees, fences, fire hydrants, pavement lines, field lines, ditches and forest lines.

- Use pylons, backpacks or skipping ropes to establish boundaries where no natural landmarks exist.
- After establishing the boundaries, have all players point to them.
- Have one or more players run the perimeter of the playing area.

Fox in the Henhouse

PLAYERS At least 10, but 14 or more for the most fun

EQUIPMENT None

GAME PLAN Escape the hungry fox or eat a hen.

HOW TO PLAY

After establishing boundaries for a tag-sized game, choose It (the Fox) and the first Hen.

Have the remaining players (the Hens) pair up and link arms at the elbows to form Henhouses. If you have an odd group of participants, you may be able to still be able to form Henhouses of the same number by having groups of three.

Have the Henhouses space themselves out throughout the playing area. The game begins with the Fox and the Hen at opposite corners of the playing area.

The Fox chases the Hen and attempts to tag her. The Hen can escape the Fox by joining a Henhouse. If a Hen links onto a Henhouse, the player whose arm they do not grab becomes the Hen and is then chased by the Fox.

For example, Foxy is chasing Hilda, and Hilda grabs onto Henry's arm. Henry had his arms linked with Harold, but since there is only room for two Hens per house, Harold must leave to be chased by Foxy.

If the Fox successfully tags a Hen, the tagged player becomes It. The ex-Fox then kicks a Hen out of her house from the opposite end of the playing area, and the chase begins again. The game is over when peaked.

VARIATIONS

This game can be renamed to fit virtually any theme that involves one group of characters against another.

Giants, Wizards, Elves

PLAYERS At least 8, but 12 or more is the most fun

EQUIPMENT None

GAME PLAN Capture all mystical forces on one team through a large group chasing game.

HOW TO PLAY

Establish boundaries for play in a rectangular area, around the size of half a basketball court. Two of these boundaries should face each other and should be visible to all players: when a player passes those lines, they are in the safe zone.

Divide the group into two even teams and have them line up along their safe line facing each other.

Explain that they are in a magic forest where ancient mystical Giants, Wizards and Elves battle for supremacy.

Explain that the Giants always defeat the Elves because they can step on them. The Wizards always defeat the Giants because of their magic powers. The Elves always defeat the Wizards because Elves are such tricky, scheming little creatures. Then teach the players the actions that go with each of the creatures.

- To pretend to be Giants, players stand on their tiptoes with their arms above their heads.

- To pretend to be Wizards, players point their hands straight out and wiggle their fingers as if they are casting a spell.

- To pretend to be Elves, players crouch and hold their hands up to their ears to make pointed Elf ears.

After you have practiced making the various actions, and after the players have an understanding of who defeats who, have the two teams huddle up separately. Each team must pick a first action and a second action – Giants and Elves, for example, or Giants and Giants. (We pick two actions in case the first actions of both teams are the same.)

The players move from their safe zone and line up facing each other a few feet apart in the middle of the playing area. When the leader calls, "Go," each team must perform their action.

The winning team must chase the losing team back to the losing team's safe zone. For example, the Wizards would chase the Giants back to the Giants' safe zone, or the Elves would chase the Wizards to the Wizards' safe zone.

Any players tagged by the winning team cross over to the other side. Between chases, allow between 10 and 20 seconds for strategizing in the huddle. If both teams choose the same first action, it is a stalemate and the second action is performed on the call of the leader.

NOTE Did you notice the resemblance between this game and Rock, Paper, Scissors? See page 98.

Chocolate Factory

PLAYERS At least 6, but best with 10 or more

EQUIPMENT None

GAME PLAN Avoid being caught by Willy Wonka and his Oompa-Loompas.

HOW TO PLAY

Choose one player or assign yourself to be Willy Wonka (It). Give all other players one of three names (or more, depending on the group size) of chocolate snacks – for example, Kit Kat, Mars Bar and Smarties.

Begin with Willy Wonka standing in the center of a large playing field with two distinct boundaries at either end.

Have everyone except Willy Wonka line up along one edge of the field. Willy Wonka then calls out one of the chocolate snacks, and everyone assigned that name has to run from one end of the field to the other.

If a player is tagged by Willy Wonka before she reaches the other end, she becomes an Oompa Loompa, one of his henchmen, and must stay in the spot where she was tagged, squatting and ready to tag players as they run past in the next round.

While Willy Wonka is allowed to move around the playing field to tag others, Oompa Loompas are stationary and only allowed to stretch their arms to tag others. Willy Wonka can then call out one (or more) chocolate snacks, and the game continues.

Things really get crazy when Willy Wonka calls out, "Chocolate Factory!" because all players still not Oompa Loompas must dash across the playing field at once, trying to get to the other side safely.

VARIATIONS

See Candy Corners and Octopus, right.

MODIFICATIONS

To increase the difficulty, allow Oompa Loompas to move about the playing field to tag others. However, they must move while still in a squatting position!

Candy Corners

PLAYERS At least 6, but best with 10 or more

EQUIPMENT None

GAME PLAN Get to the Candy Corners faster than your competitors.

HOW TO PLAY

Establish four landmarks in your playing area. These can either be four objects (backpacks, pylons, beanbags, fire hydrants, skipping ropes), or the north, south, east and west walls of your room.

Have the players list off some of their favorite junk food or candy: jelly beans, ju-jubes, chocolate, sour keys, licorice and bubblegum are some examples.

Name your four points after four different types of candy. When you call out a type of candy, all players must run to that point. For example, if the south wall is Jelly Bean, when you call out "Jelly Bean," all players must run to that wall. After a few practice rounds, the last player to get to the wall is "out."

To psych players out, call the point that they are already at. For example, if the players are at the Chocolate pavement line, call out "Chocolate." Any players that flinch or begin to run to another point are "out." To add an element of chaos, call "Candy Factory" and have all players run to the middle of the playing field.

VARIATIONS

Add more than four types of candy to increase the difficulty level.

To play without elimination, allow players to rejoin the game after two or three rounds of being "out."

You can also combine this game with games like Ship to Shore (page 114) to include actions. For example, "Stir the Sugar" could be a twisting dance that players perform in whatever Candy Corner they happen to be in.

Octopus
(aka Run Like Chewbacca)

PLAYERS At least 6, but best with 10 or more

EQUIPMENT None

GAME PLAN Run across the "ocean floor" without being tagged by the octopus and turned to seaweed.

HOW TO PLAY

Establish rectangular boundaries based on the size of your group and their running abilities: the larger the group, the larger the playing field. The size of a basketball court will do for games with approximately 20 players.

Pick one or two players to be the Octopus and have them stand in the middle of the playing area. The other players line up along one side of the boundaries and face the Octopus (or Octopi).

When either the leader or the Octopus call, "Octopus," all players must run from one side of the area to the other without being tagged by the Octopus.

When players are tagged, they become "seaweed" and must stand in place and try to tag other players as they run by them. The game increases in complexity as players must evade the Octopus and dodge the seaweed.

The last player tagged is the next Octopus.

Older veteran players will discover the strategy of hanging back along the starting point and trying to deke out the Octopus. To avoid extended stalemates, we suggest having a 5-to-10-second limit before the Octopus can attack players hanging around the starting point, rather than having an Octopus-free zone.

VARIATIONS

Octopus is one of the easiest games to modify for a theme. Simply pick one character to be the chaser or villain (Octopus), one type of character to be the minion (seaweed), and one type of character to be the hero (player).

One of our all-time favorite variations of Octopus is Run Like Chewbacca, invented by one of our camp colleagues, Acuma. In his variation, the Octopus is Darth Vader, the seaweeds are Stormtroopers, and the players must run across the playing field while yelling like the furry character Chewbacca from *Star Wars*. This loud and silly variation is a hit with many of our younger campers, who enjoy yodeling and hollering as they dodge the evil Darth Vader.

If you want to play a game like Octopus in the pool or the lake, check out Fisherman (page 154).

NOTE This is a much safer and more camp and school appropriate version of the old game British Bulldog (page 127).

TRADITIONAL GAMES

Times have changed, and safety and childcare practices too! Out of principle, we have not included games that encourage children to pummel their playmates. Your grandfathers might have played games such as Cockfighting or the "Games for Strength" (such as Wrist-Pushing, Wrestling and Kneel to Your Superior) that were in Sir Robert Baden Powell's original *Scouting Games*, but very few of those games would be approved of by parents, camp supervisors, coaches, educators or scout leaders today.

However, a number of old-fashioned games that sometimes involve displays of physical assertiveness or strength can still be played, as long they are correctly supervised, limits are set, and participants are matched in strength and ability. The occasional scraped knee or bruised elbow may occur, but nobody should get hurt so much that it isn't fun for all.

Capture the Flag

PLAYERS At least 8 for small spaces, but for the most fun, 15 or more in a large space

EQUIPMENT Two sets of flags (can be pinnies, fabric, beanbags or anything players can hide easily)

GAME PLAN Capture the opposing team's flag or flags and return them to your own home base before they capture yours.

HOW TO PLAY

Choose a large space and divide the group up into two teams. Establish a clear center line and have each team stand in their zone. After you explain the rules of the game, have the teams hide their flags somewhere in their zone and have them establish a home base where they will keep the captured flags.

When the game begins, both teams try to capture the flags of the other team. For a flag to be successfully captured, it must be carried back to the attacking team's home base.

The defending team can tag attacking players when they are in the defensive zone. If the attacking player escapes with the flag back to their own zone, the defensive players cannot tag them.

Tagged players must stand by you, as leader, in a neutral area for a count of 20 before rejoining the game or are they imprisoned (see variations).

As an added complication, you could allow players to "free" flags from the opposing team's home base, but this will prolong the game. Alternatively, you can direct players to return their flag directly to you rather than to their home base.

The game is over when all flags are captured or when the game is peaked. If you peak the game before a clear winner is established, the team with the most flags wins.

VARIATIONS

Instead of having players come to the leader and count to 20 when they are tagged, have them stand in "prison" behind the enemy's flags. They can then be freed by a direct tag from their own teammate. This complicates the strategy, as the opposing team must choose whether to protect a flag or an imprisoned player.

To establish a clear winner sooner, give attacking players immunity from being tagged as soon as they are in possession of the flag rather than waiting until they cross the line back into their own zone.

For a hide and seek variation, play in a wooded area with fewer flags and using imprisonment.

For gymnasiums or other highly visible spaces, increase the number of flags and place them in a line to eliminate the challenge of looking for the flag.

King of the Castle

PLAYERS At least 3, no more than 8

EQUIPMENT A good location

GAME PLAN Become the King (or Queen) of the castle and stay there.

HOW TO PLAY

Find a small hill or other location, such as a tree stump or snowbank, where one player can stand higher than all the others and yet be pulled down safely. This is the castle.

Choose a player, say Patrick, to be the first King of the Castle. He gets to stand on top of the castle and signal the start of the game. Then the other players have to try to get Patrick down from the castle and take his place. There will be pulling, pushing and shoving, but your players should be able to keep themselves under control so that no one gets hurt!

As soon as Cam takes Patrick's place, then he becomes the new King, and all the other players will now be trying to pull Cam down to take his place! The game continues either for a set period of time or until you decide the players have had enough.

Red Rover

PLAYERS At least 8, best with a large group

EQUIPMENT None

GAME PLAN Capture your opponents or break through the opposing team's line.

HOW TO PLAY

Divide your group into two teams and choose one team to go first. They choose a player from the other team to challenge. The teams stand in lines facing each other about 20 feet apart, each player holding the hand or wrist of each person beside him or her.

The challenging team then sings out to the other team, "Red Rover, Red Rover, we call Sally over." Sally has to leave her team and run at the challenging team's line between two players in an attempt try to break their arms apart. If Sally gets through the line, she brings back to her own team's line one of the two players whose arms she broke through. If she doesn't, she is captured and has to join the challenging team.

The other team then challenges a player, "Red Rover, Red Rover, we call Umai over..." and play continues with teams alternating turns until one team has most (or all) of the players. In fact, if all the players are on one team, then everybody is a winner.

British Bulldog

PLAYERS At least 5, more is better

EQUIPMENT None

GAME PLAN Be the last player captured.

HOW TO PLAY

Divide players into two teams. Define the boundaries of your playing field with two lines about 30 feet apart and sidelines. Choose one person to be the Bulldog. All the other players line up on one side of the playing field, and the Bulldog stands in the middle of the two lines.

The game starts when the Bulldog calls out, "British bulldog!" Everyone has to cross the field without going out of bounds or getting caught. Players captured by the Bulldog become Bulldogs when he lifts them up in the air and shouts, "One, two, three, British bulldog!"

Everyone who makes it across is safe and lines up for the next round. Play continues until there is only one player left not captured. That person gets to be the first Bulldog in the next game.

Cops and Robbers

PLAYERS 8 or more

EQUIPMENT None

GAME PLAN Avoid the Cops and free your fellow Robbers, or keep all those pesky Robbers in jail.

HOW TO PLAY

In this tag-and-capture game, two groups of players – the Cops and the Robbers – try to outsmart and outrun each other.

Establish boundaries and divide the group into two even teams. If you have odd numbers, it is best to place the extra player on the side of the Robbers.

Establish a landmark (tree, backpack, pylon, spot along a wall) that will serve as the prison. Some leaders also like to pick a Robber or two to start in prison, so that the other Robbers are forced to go near the Cops.

The game begins with the Cops and Robbers on either side of the playing field. The Cops must tag the Robbers and bring them back to prison. The Robbers must avoid the Cops and must also free their fellow Robbers from prison by creating a "jail break."

A jail break happens when a Robber tags either the prison landmark or the Robbers in prison. To make jail breaks possible, create a "no jail-keepers" rules so that Cops must stand 5 to 10 feet away from the jail from all times.

The game is over when all the Robbers are captured, when all the Robbers are freed, or when the game is peaked.

VARIATIONS

In the Double-Capture variation of Cops and Robbers, the Robbers also have a lair in which they can capture Cops who have strayed too far into enemy territory. For this variation, you should divide the playing area in two and play with Capture the Flag-style rules (page 126). You should also begin the game with a Cop in the Robbers' lair and a Robber in prison, so that teams have a reason to go into each other's territory.

Supervision and Safety

Many camp programs, recreation programs and schools are increasing their safety requirements, often at the request of concerned parents. Games such as Hide and Seek and Capture the Flag played in woods and fields may evoke nostalgic images of what camp is "supposed" to be like, but supervision and safety concerns often make these games unplayable, particularly for larger camps and schools.

Not being able to see all of the children in your charge at all times is a serious safety risk, and one that should not be taken without consideration of all the possible dangers. Threats can include bullying, sexual predators and abduction, injury (and the ensuing liability) and anaphylactic or allergic reactions.

Before you plan an activity where you will not be able to supervise all children at all times, consider the following questions. Many of these are especially applicable to camps, but they are all points you should consider whether you are a camp leader or director, a sports coach, teacher, parent, babysitter or even a big sister.

- What are your program's policies on supervision, safety and liability? Do you have liability insurance? Is direct supervision at all times a stipulation of that insurance?

Predator Prey

PLAYERS At least 8, but 12 or more for maximum fun

EQUIPMENT None

GAME PLAN Eat your prey and avoid being eaten by your predators.

HOW TO PLAY

Establish boundaries for play in a rectangular area approximately the size of half a basketball court. At either end of the playing area, mark out two lines (with pylons, backpacks, skipping rope or an invisible line). When a player passes those lines, they are in the safe zone.

Divide the group into two even teams and have them line up in the middle of the playing field facing each other with their backs to their own safe zone.

Tell the group that in the animal kingdom, there are predators (the eaters) and there are prey (the eaten). Some animals, like spiders, both eat (small bugs) and are eaten (birds).

Explain that you will be telling each team what animal they are. Whichever team is the predator will chase the prey team members back to their safe zone. Any tagged prey must join the predator team for the next round.

For example, if you call out, "Cat and Mouse," all the Cats chase all the Mice back to the Mice safe zone. Or if you call out, "Cat and Dog," the Dogs chase the Cats back to the Cat safe zone.

The best part of this game is watching the players figure out who eats who, especially when you get to tricky combinations such as Human versus Lion, or Mouse versus Elephant.

- Do you have exclusive access to your site? Is your location isolated enough so that any strange faces will stand out? Does your group have regular interaction with community members? Do you have fences? Single or multiple entry points?
- If you are near a forest or a wooded area, are the paths in the forest clearly marked and easy to walk on? Are there obvious boundary markers that would make it easy for players to recognize when they have gone too far?
- Do you have players in your group who have not been getting along? Has bullying been a problem, particularly at less structured times such as lunch or recess? Do you have children in your group who fight?
- Do you have children in your group with special needs? Children who are uncomfortable with change or need structure in their daily programs?
- Do you have children with severe allergies? Are they allergic to peanuts or bees or any other foods, substances or animals? Do they carry an Epipen?

If you cannot confidently say you have addressed all these questions with well-considered and positive precautions and safeguards, then change your program to ensure all children will remain safe.

Stay Safe in Sticky Situations

- Go over safety rules with your kids as part of their introduction to the program. Point out boundaries and out-of-bounds areas and tell them what to do if they need help. Some children will understand best if you role-play situations.
- Do a quick visual check of any new site, including a check for hazards on the ground and suspicious people in the area.
- If you see someone suspicious, wave hello to them. Be friendly and ask them if you can help them with something. Most "bad people" will be scared away by your friendly approach.
- If you ever feel unsafe, leave an area.
- Take a first-aid course and keep your certification up to date.
- Make sure all your co-workers and volunteers know your program's safety standards, bathroom policy and supervision policy, what to do if a child gets injured, and how to search for any children.
- Never leave an injured child alone. Although many camps have a hands-off policy, it is sometimes better to carry an injured child carefully to get help than it is to leave the injured child or to send other children back to get help. This is particularly important in wooded areas, where tripping over a tree root can lead to a broken leg. You would hate to send a child to get help and end up having two twisted ankles instead of one. (Good first-aid training will help you assess the situation and formulate the appropriate response.)
- Before entering rooms in any facility you use (including bathrooms and change rooms), call "Hello." If you do not get an answer, do a quick visual check before you send the children in. If someone is in there, you can either send the kids in, saying, "I'm sending some kids in to use the room," or you can wait until the bathroom or change room is empty.
- If you ever decide to send children by themselves to the bathroom or to run an errand, consider using a buddy system. This is particularly useful in unfamiliar sites.

Chicken Fight

PLAYERS 8 or more

EQUIPMENT Two pieces of fabric (for example, pinnies)

GAME PLAN With only one hand and one leg to use, steal your opponent's piece of fabric before they steal yours.

HOW TO PLAY

Have players seated in a circle with a large space in the middle.

Select two players to tuck a piece of fabric into the back of their shorts (or clothespin the fabric on).

With one hand holding one leg bent behind them, and hopping, they must try to seize the other player's fabric with their free hand.

The winner can continue and face off against a new opponent, or two new players can be picked for a new round of fighting.

Sword in the Stone: Supreme Master of the Universe

PLAYERS At least 12 or more; best with large groups

EQUIPMENT A hula hoop and either a short foam sword, a half pool noodle or even a rolled-up newspaper.

GAME PLAN Put the sword back in the stone if you are It; be the Supreme Master of the Universe if you are not.

HOW TO PLAY

Have the group stand in a large circle, arm's length apart and choose one player to be the first It.

Place the "stone" (hula hoop) in the middle of the circle and give It the "sword" (half pool noodle, foam sword or a rolled-up newspaper).

While It walks around the circle, the other players swap places in the circle behind his back. They are not allowed to swap places with their neighbors – the person on either side of them – so they must take a risk, make eye contact with another player, and race to switch places.

If It sees a player swapping places, It races toward that player and tags her below the waist with the "sword." It must tag the other player while she is in the middle of switching places. Once she is in place back in the circle, It may not tag her.

If It tags the other player successfully, It races back to replace the "sword" in the "stone." The other player then can try to pick up the sword and tag the previous It before he gets back to the open space, or she can begin trying to tag other players.

For example, when Ethan is It, he catches Kelsey and Hannah switching places. Ethan tags Hannah before she gets back to her spot in the circle. Ethan then places the sword back in the stone and turns to run back to the empty space. Hannah picks up the sword and tries to tag Ethan before he gets back into place. If Hannah can tag Ethan, she replaces the sword in the stone and races back to her original spot. If Hannah cannot tag Ethan, she becomes It and the game continues.

Once the players have got the hang of the game, introduce the "Supreme Master of the Universe" challenge. Instead of merely swapping places with other players, really bold players can run into the center of the circle, assume a push-up position, yell, "I am the Supreme Master of the Universe," and run back to their spot in the circle without being tagged. You can award points for players who are able to accomplish this miraculous feat!

VARIATIONS

Introduce a second or third sword to increase the chaos level. For a more junior introduction to the swapping skills required in this game, try playing Kitty Wants a Corner (page 83).

Or play without switching places. The person in the middle hits a player in the circle (below the waist) and then goes back to the center.

MODIFICATIONS

For groups who have difficulty understanding personal space or who are super-competitive, we suggest using hula hoops as place-keepers for the circle.

NOTE While this game seems complicated, it is Mary's favorite game of all time. She likes playing it with 20 or more people, a circle the size of a basketball court, and at least two swords. She has also won the title of Supreme Master of the Universe on several occasions.

Hide and Seek

PLAYERS Any number, but best with 4 or more

EQUIPMENT None

GAME PLAN Pick a spot to hide from It.

HOW TO PLAY

Establish clear boundaries where players can hide (for example, within a fenced area or only "five baby steps" into the forest).

Choose one player to be It. (See How to Choose It, page 118.)

Have It close her eyes and count to a prearranged number. Depending on the size of the playing field, the number may be large or small. We like to spice things up by having It count in slow motion, or on fast forward. For example, if we say, "Count to 100 on fast forward," It will count all the way to 100 but very quickly.

While It is counting, all the remaining players go to find hiding spots within the boundaries.

Once It is finished counting, she must shout out, "Ready or not, here I come!" and then search for the hidden players, continuing to search until all players are found.

The first player to be found is It for the next round.

VARIATIONS

In a variation of Hide and Seek commonly known as Sardines, only one player goes to hide, while the remaining players count together to the prearranged number. When they are finished, they call out, "Ready or not, here we come!" and individually search for the player. When a searching player discovers the hidden player, she joins him in his hiding spot and any additional searching players who discover the hiding spot also hide there. The last player to find the hiding spot is It for the next round.

MODIFICATIONS

To increase the activity level and make it more challenging, encourage players to switch hiding spots during the game.

Or, at the beginning of the game, designate an area to be a "home free." Then, when It discovers a hidden player, she must tag them rather than just finding them to eliminate them from the game. Upon being discovered, the hidden player has the opportunity to make a dash for "home-free." If It cannot tag him before he reaches home free, the hidden player is safe.

Supervision and Hide and Seek

After a long battle with ourselves, we decided to include Hide and Seek. It is a brilliantly fun game and has stood the test of time. It incorporates speed, strategy, observation and intuition, and is one of the most inclusive games out there: any child can hide with a little bit of help. However, the "hide" part of Hide and Seek is troubling for many camp programs that have constant supervision policies, and unfortunately we have never been able to play Hide and Seek at camp because the programs we worked at required that we be able to see the campers at all times.

However, if yours is a program with a relaxed supervision policy, or if you are a parent or babysitter with a big backyard that is safe and familiar for the kids, by all means, play Hide and Seek. Just establish boundaries such as "don't go beyond the fire hydrants" or "stay close enough that you can hear It count," and tell the kids to call for help if they trip or otherwise get hurt.

Lost Child

No matter how many safeguards you have in place, there may come a day when a child in your care goes missing. The important thing at that point is to have a system in place that will allow you to deal with the problem.

At some camp programs, the first step if you lose a child is to search the surrounding area and tell other leaders and supervisors. Then you might have other leaders stop and count their children. Often times, a child will have simply wandered from one group to the next.

After that, it is a good idea to bring all the other children to a central location with a few staff while the remaining staff do a more thorough search of the area. Some camps use walkie talkies or cell phones to communicate, but in other situations shouting has to do the trick.

Check with other programs in your area. They will be happy to lend your their emergency policy, which you can use as a guideline and adapt for your own site.

It's also advisable, as with any other mishap or out-of-the-ordinary event, to report to parents and any other concerned individuals at the end of the day if a child goes missing, even for the shortest period of time. It's best to be up front and work together on ways to make sure it doesn't happen again.

What Time Is It, Mr. Wolf?

PLAYERS 6 or more

EQUIPMENT None

GAME PLAN Make it back without being Mr. Wolf's lunch!

HOW TO PLAY

Choose one player to be Mr. Wolf. Have him stand at one end of the playing field, facing away from all the players.

The other players line up at the opposite end of the field, facing Mr. Wolf. Have them say in unison, "What time is it, Mr. Wolf?" And Mr. Wolf will respond with a time, for example, "Three o'clock!"

The players then must take three steps forward. Again, they will ask, "What time is it, Mr. Wolf?" And Mr. Wolf will continue to give them times (up to 12 o'clock), and the players will continue to take the same number of steps as the time.

When Mr. Wolf senses that some players are close at hand, instead of saying something-o'clock, he can shout, "Lunch Time!" and all players must dash back to the starting point while trying to avoid being Mr. Wolf's lunch. The first person Mr. Wolf tags becomes Mr. Wolf in the next round.

NOTE This game can be used to help teach younger players how to tell time on an analog clock. Instead of Mr. Wolf shouting out the time, he can use an oversized paper clock to turn the time. The players must read the time and when prompted shout in unison the number of steps as they take them, ending with "o'clock." (For example, "One, two, three, four o'clock!")

Streets and Alleys

PLAYERS 16 or more

EQUIPMENT None

GAME PLAN Tag the runner or avoid being tagged while running down streets and alleys.

HOW TO PLAY

Choose one player to be It and one player to be the runner.

Then have the rest of your group line up side by side in rows with an equal number of players in each row. For instance, if you have 18 players in all, you will have 16 players in the rest of the group, so you could have four rows of four. If you have 20 players in all, you could have three rows of six. See the illustration.

Have the players in each row join hands.

Pick one of the players in the rows to be the caller, or choose to be the caller yourself if you are lined up.

The caller will have a lot of say in directing the play of the game.

Meanwhile, It has to try to tag the runner, so she will start chasing the runner up and down and around through the rows.

However, the caller can at any time yell, "Streets," and all the players have to let go of the players beside them and switch position, turning a quarter turn, to hold hands with the players in front of and behind them instead. When they do that, It and the runner will have to change direction too, and run crosswise to where they were running before.

At any time the caller can call out, "Alleys," and all the players in rows have to turn again to hold hands with the players in front of and behind them. That means It and the runner will have to change direction again because the Alleys run perpendicular to the Streets!

As the caller keeps on calling "Streets" and "Alleys," all the changing direction makes it harder for both It and the runner.

When It finally catches the runner, the runner can become It or you can choose a new It along with a new runner and caller.

This game ends best if you peak it when everyone is still having fun.

Ultimate Frisbee

PLAYERS 6 or more

EQUIPMENT A Frisbee

GAME PLAN Score a goal by catching the Frisbee beyond your opponent's goal line.

HOW TO PLAY

This game requires a fairly large space, depending on the players' throwing ability. Form two equal teams and decide which team will receive the Frisbee first. Have both teams line up behind a marked goal line.

One team begins the game by tossing the Frisbee downfield toward the receiving team. This team will take the Frisbee and pass it to a teammate on his or her way to their opponent's goal. However, the Frisbee can only be brought toward the goal by throwing it.

Once a player catches the Frisbee, she can only pivot (keeping one foot stationary) before throwing it again. We especially like this rule because it encourages cooperation and equal play among teammates, and one player cannot dominate the field.

Play continues until a player misses a pass (and the Frisbee touches the ground) or the Frisbee is intercepted, and then possession is given to the other team.

A point is awarded when a player successfully passes the Frisbee from outside the opposing team's goal line to a teammate who is standing inside the goal line. Each goal is worth one point, and Ultimate Frisbee can be played up to a certain number of points (for example, first to 10 goals) or within a time limit. As always, we encourage peaking the game.

Dealing with Boring Betty, Competitive Charlie and Lazy Linda: Encouraging Equal Play

• Play the game yourself. This way you can encourage participation and model how to be a good sport.

• Discuss the concept of teamwork with your group. We use the metaphor of a Greek phalanx: everyone works together to protect everyone else. For a less violent comparison, bring up the idea of a power play in hockey: when one player lets down the team and takes a penalty, the whole team suffers.

• Find out what everyone's favorite game, sport or activity is on the first day of the program. If possible, promise that you will try to play everyone's favorite game on the condition that they participate in the program activities. If Boring Betty refuses to even try to play Human Ladders (page 97), the group won't play her favorite, Up Jenkins (page 61).

• Have a "must try" policy: all participants must try the activity for the first five minutes (or 10 minutes). If after that time, they still don't want to play, then they can sit quietly. Try not to be overly chatty with players who are not participating. Your attention should not be a reward for lack of participation.

• Five or 10 minutes into each game, remind all participants to involve everyone. We shout, "Make sure everyone has a turn" to remind our players.

• Praise your Competitive Charlies privately for their exceptional athletic abilities. You might even tell them that they have coaching potential. What you need is to see them encouraging and training other teammates so that they can get better at the game. This type of positive reinforcement will get better results than just telling Charlie to calm down and share the ball.

• If Competitive Charlie gets aggressive, you can absolutely give him a time-out. Explain that you need him to cool off: you know he is frustrated because he isn't winning or his team isn't succeeding, but that safety is more important than victory.

• Never give time-outs for lack of participation. If Lazy Linda doesn't want to play tag, giving her a time-out is only giving her what she wants.

• Acknowledge when any of your players "step outside their comfort zone" by playing the game and pushing themselves, or by backing off and encouraging their team. The best type of praise is sincere and specific ("Hey, Charlie, I really liked it when you passed the ball to William. That was great teamwork") rather than vague and generic ("Good game, Charlie").

Foosball Soccer

PLAYERS 8 or more

EQUIPMENT Ball, net markers

GAME PLAN Score a goal on your opponent's net without leaving your position

HOW TO PLAY

Foosball is a table-top version of soccer where lines of toy soccer players are controlled by one or two players to score a goal. This is an attempt at a real-life version of the popular table game.

If you have a gymnasium with lines (or any floor with horizontal and vertical lines), have the teams arrange themselves on the lines and set up two nets. If you're not in that situation, just arrange players in lines yourself, keeping an eye to make sure the lines stay straight and players don't stray from their positions. Each player must restrict themselves to the one line, and teams must try and score on their opponent's net without leaving their lines. Players are allowed to pass the ball down their own line or to another one of their lines.

This game is best played in a smaller space with walls for the ball to bounce off. If the ball stops out of reach of the players, the leader brings the ball back to the middle or gives the ball to one team (alternating between teams to keep things even).

Dodgeball

PLAYERS At least 6, but best with 10 or more

EQUIPMENT One ball (or more, for added challenge)

GAME PLAN Dodge a ball coming your way, but try to make your throws on target.

HOW TO PLAY

Divide the group into two teams and place them on either side of a playing field with a center divider clearly marked (or pointed out to the group).

Have teams line up at the far end of their area and place a ball (or more than one) along the center line.

On your call, teams will race to grab the balls in the middle. Immediately, they can begin aiming them at players on the opposing team.

They must not pass the center line under any circumstances, including trying to grab a wayward ball. Any player who is hit below the waist is out. Any player whose throw is caught by the opposing team (with no bounce in between) is also out.

VARIATIONS

If you are looking for ways to keep players in the game longer, consider playing a non-elimination version of Dodgeball, like King's Court (page 140).

Alternatively, you can have each team assign a "Doctor." Each team only gets one Doctor, and this Doctor has the power to heal eliminated players. When hit, players simply sit down on the playing field. The Doctor will try to covertly tap them on the head to heal them and allow them to rejoin the game. However, if the Doctor is hit below the waist, the team will have no one to heal their eliminated players and must survive without a Doctor.

Often, if players are clever enough, they'll have decoy Doctors that walk with the real Doctor and also tap players on the head (so the opposing team has difficulty targeting the real Doctor).

MODIFICATIONS

Instead of placing the balls along the center line, you can also just give each team a ball or two. But we enjoy the dash for the center by those bold enough to get close to the other team.

If you are playing with participants who may be slow runners (or if they can throw quite far), it's best to play in an enclosed space; that way, half the game isn't spent chasing after wayward balls.

There's More to Life Than Circle Dodgeball

Circle Dodgeball: some love it but we do not. It's usually unimaginative, mindless and repetitive. It seems to us that it is overplayed in every camp. The kids sit in a circle. You pick one or two players to stand in the middle of the circle. You give a ball to somebody sitting in the circle and that player throws it at the kids in the middle, who must dodge the ball. If they get hit below the waist, they switch places with the person who hit them. You can vary the number of players and balls.

If you're going to play it, this game is best used when participants are arriving or leaving for the day, as it is flexible in the number of players. As is, it doesn't promote cooperation or teamwork unless the leader specifically modifies it. Here, we've done the modifying for you.

The game 007 Dodgeball includes the same elements of Circle Dodgeball that kids love but it helps build interdependence on a team and has that extra element that keeps leaders and players interested. Dragonball (page 140) does the same thing, taking basic Circle Dodgeball and adding team participation and complexity to challenge campers beyond the endless hit-switch-hit-switch of the original.

007 Dodgeball

PLAYERS 6 or more

EQUIPMENT One ball
(or more, for added challenge)

GAME PLAN Try to hit the player in the middle with three shots (and wait to reload).

HOW TO PLAY

This game is a combination of a popular hand-clap game (007) and Dodgeball.

In the handclap game (see below), players only have a certain number of "shots" before reloading. The idea is the same here. Have players sit cross-legged in a circle with one player chosen to go in the middle. Players will try to hit the player in the middle below the waist with the ball.

To prevent certain players from getting the ball more often than others, and thus to encourage cooperation among the group, 007 Dodgeball incorporates a reloading system.

For example, if Anna throws the ball once, she must hold one hand up in the air until she gets the ball again. After Anna throws her second shot, she must put both hands up in the air until she gets the ball again. After Anna's third throw, she puts both hands on her head and cannot reload (and throw another pass) until the player in the middle is hit below the waist by another player or until you direct all players to reload and join the game again. Players will know they cannot pass the ball to Anna because she has both hands on her head.

If Anna is successful in hitting the player in the middle on one of her three shots, she becomes the player in the middle.

VARIATIONS

If you find the middle player gets out too quickly to have an effect on sharing the passing among the group, don't allow everyone to reload after a change in the middle player. Instead, instruct players to reload on your call.

Sometimes we include a beanbag, and the leader will toss it to players to allow them to reload mid-game.

MODIFICATIONS

To encourage more interdependence on your team, consider limiting the number of throw attempts even further, and have players reload after two shots instead of three.

007 Clap Game

007 is a popular clapping game in our neck of the woods. Players face each other, and slap their thighs twice in rhythm, chanting "Double-Oh-Seven." After saying, "Double-Oh-Seven," they must perform one of three actions:

- shooting (finger guns pointed at opposite player),
- blocking (arms crossed in front of body), or
- reloading (thumbs pointed behind you, over the shoulders).

Players cannot shoot without "bullets," which are gained when reloading (one bullet per "reload" movement.)

Players win the round by shooting while the opposing player is reloading (and left unguarded). If both players shoot, neither gains anything, as they cancel each other out. If the opposing player is "blocking," shots cannot get through.

Players rarely keep track of who wins or loses, and it's a great way for players to pass the time while waiting for others to finish lunch, or on a long bus ride to the zoo.

King's Court Dodgeball

PLAYERS Best with 12 or more

EQUIPMENT One ball (or more for added challenge)

GAME PLAN Get as many players of the other team, while keeping your own team in the game.

HOW TO PLAY

Divide the group into two equal teams and divide a playing area into two, each team with their own side. Behind each team's area is a marked box (usually the width of the area but much smaller). This is the Dungeon of the each team's King's Court.

Each team begins the game at the far end of their area. Place one or more soft balls (like utility balls) along the center line between the two areas.

At your signal, both teams must race to be the first to grab a ball. Immediately, players can begin throwing their balls at players on the opposing team.

If a player catches a throw (with no bounce between), the thrower must go to the opposing team's Dungeon. If a player is hit below the waist, the hit player must go to the opposing team's Dungeon. If a player is hit above the waist, the person who threw the ball has to go to the other team's Dungeon.

While in the opposing team's Dungeon, players can try to catch stray balls, or encourage their own team to throw them the ball. This is because players in the Dungeon can also take aim at the opposing team – which is what makes the game more challenging. Players have to watch in front and behind them to dodge incoming balls. It also makes it more inclusive, because players are never eliminated from the game. If someone in the Dungeon hits a player on the opposing team below the waist, they are released from the Dungeon and can return to their own team's area.

The game ends when all players of one team are in their opposing team's Dungeon or when the game is peaked.

Dragonball

PLAYERS 12 or more

EQUIPMENT One ball (or more for added challenge)

GAME PLAN Tag the front of the dragon, or if you're part of the dragon, dodge the ball!

HOW TO PLAY

This is similar to Circle Dodgeball but adds an exciting team element to an otherwise regular game. Pick four members of the group – they will join together (one behind the other, holding on to each other's shoulders) – to create the Dragon.

Have the other players create a circle surrounding the Dragon. Give one member of the circle a soft ball (like a utility ball). The players in the circle will try to hit the front member of the Dragon, while the other members of the Dragon will twist and turn to block the front player from being hit. This is because once the front player is hit (below the waist) he or she must sit down and the person who successfully threw the ball becomes the back of the Dragon. Everyone else in the Dragon then moves up and becomes that much closer to leaving the Dragon's tail.

MODIFICATIONS

The Dragon can vary in size depending on the group. If there are participants who may need guidance, you can also have players assigned in pairs. Then, if the front two players are hit, they both have to break off the Dragon, and the two players who hit the first two become the next "pair" to join the Dragon.

Ball Master

PLAYERS The more, the better

EQUIPMENT Several utility balls

GAME PLAN Hit other players below the waist with a ball and avoid being hit yourself.

HOW TO PLAY

This is an every-man-for-himself version of Dodgeball: there are no teams. Have players scatter themselves in an open space and toss in a number of balls. The more people, the more balls you will need.

Players who are holding a ball are allowed to take three steps before aiming the ball below another player's waist. If a player is hit (below the waist), she is out, and must sit on the sidelines. However, she can return to the game when the player who got her out is hit.

For example, if Scott has the ball and hits Lindsay below the waist, she is out of the game until another player throws and hits Scott below the waist. Make sure to explain this rule beforehand and confirm that everyone understands – otherwise you may end up with several players sitting on the side who are actually back in the game.

We like Ball Master because unlike other versions of Dodgeball, there's less focus on elimination, and the more talented a player is, the more likely they'll have trouble staying in the game. It challenges the most talented while including those who need a little help.

The game ends when it is peaked, or in the unlikely situation that only one player remains on the field. We recommend peaking the game.

VARIATIONS

If your players tend to hit above the waist, have those who hit above the waist also eliminated until the person they wrongly hit are out. (If Scott hits Lindsay above the waist, he is out until Lindsay is hit below the waist by another player.)

Modifying Games for Number of Participants

- Use team rotation or first and second strings.
- Increase the number of balls in play.
- Expand or reduce the playing field.
- Have players work as partners and link arms.
- Increase or decrease the number of outs allowed.

European Handball

PLAYERS 6 or more, preferably more than 10

EQUIPMENT Ball, net markers

GAME PLAN Score on your opposing team's net.

HOW TO PLAY

The game is played like soccer, with two teams, goalies, and the same general size of playing area, except that instead of kicking the ball, players throw it.

Begin by dividing the group into two teams, with one member of each team guarding the goal net. Choose one representative of each team to participate in a jump for possession of the ball.

The player who gains possession and is carrying the ball can take only three steps before he must toss the ball to one of his teammates. The three-step rule is designed to prevent players from hogging the ball.

Players not carrying the ball can take as many steps as they like. This allows them to get into position to catch or intercept a pass. If they catch the ball, again, they are limited to taking three steps before they must pass the ball or try and score a goal.

Players must toss the ball downfield to each other and successfully throw it into the opposing team's net to score a goal.

Possession of the ball can change after a goal has been scored, if the ball is picked up off the ground or intercepted in mid-air. Players are not allowed to forcibly take the ball from another player, and body contact is obviously discouraged.

Set a time limit, and the team with the most goals when play is up wins.

This game is a good variation of soccer to use on hot days or days when the air quality is poor. The rules are similar, but because of the restrictions on movement, players run less.

It's also a handy sport to play when you have a wider variety of abilities on a team – the three-step rule ensures cooperation on a team because passing is required regularly. This way, everyone can participate, not just more athletic players.

Speedball

PLAYERS 6 or more, preferably more than 10

EQUIPMENT Ball, net markers

GAME PLAN Score on your opposing team's net.

HOW TO PLAY

This game is a combination of soccer and European Handball. Players are divided into two teams, each with a goalie. Choose one representative from each team to participate in a jump for possession of the ball.

As in European Handball, the player with possession can take only three steps before passing the ball to a teammate. However, in Speedball, the ball can be played on the ground or in the air. The moment the ball touches the ground, the game becomes soccer, players are not restricted in their movement, and general rules of soccer apply.

The game can be converted back to the rules of European Handball if one of the players kicks the ball up in the air so another player can catch it, or if the goalie gets possession and chooses to throw the ball.

Set your own time limit for the game, and the team with the most goals when the time is up wins. Again, this game is a good variation for hot days or days when the air quality is poor, because the players run less.

Although it is more challenging than European Handball, it is still easier to play with group of players with a variety of abilities, because when the game is converted to European Handball, all players can participate equally, regardless of skill level.

Dryland Torpedo

PLAYERS Best with 10 or more

EQUIPMENT A few folding gym mats (or goal nets), some large, soft balls

GAME PLAN Make it through the ocean without being hit by an incoming torpedo.

HOW TO PLAY

Find a long space to play. Set up the gym mats, goal nets (or something that can serve as a protective "wall") so they are standing at intervals throughout the center of the space. There should be enough room for one of the teams to run between the mats, and the mats should alternate from one to the other side of the "ocean." See the illustration.

Divide the group into two equal teams. One team will be "crossing the ocean," and the other team will be launching the torpedoes. Have the first team (the Green Team) line up at one end of the ocean. Have the other team (the Blue Bombers) stand on both sides of the ocean and give them balls (torpedoes) to throw.

On your signal, the Green Team will dash between the mats, and the Blue Bombers will try to hit the Green Team players with the torpedoes. Green Team players are allowed to briefly pause behind a mat to avoid being hit with a torpedo. Usually, though, it isn't an issue, as hiding behind one mat will not protect you from the torpedoes being launched from the other side.

Once all Green Team Players have reached the other side, tally the number of players hit by the Blue Bombers' torpedoes. The Green Team will run the ocean gauntlet three more times, tallying the number of hits at the end of each turn. Then, the tables turn, and the launching team, the Blue Bombers, must run the ocean gauntlet.

Repeat the process. The team with the least number of hits against them at the end of the game wins.

MODIFICATIONS

If you're playing with slower players, consider forcing a three-second stall between each torpedo launch. Explain it as the time needed to reload a torpedo. Or consider including more or fewer balls or protective mats.

VARIATIONS

Try playing the in-water version of Torpedo (page 155) when at the pool or lake.

Wet and Wild

OH, FOR THE DAYS OF RUNNING THROUGH THE SPRINKLER! There is nothing better on a really hot summer day than getting absolutely soaked through. Tacking down a tent tarp and using a fire hose to make a gigantic Slip 'n Slide is one of our favorite, albeit somewhat dangerous, hot weather activities, something you might not choose to do — but there are plenty of other ways to play safely in, around and with water.

Many of the games in this book can be modified to be played in wading pools, or with wet sponges instead of balls. The games in this section, however, are specifically designed to be played with water. They make the most out of how water slows us down as we move through it, of water's cooling and surprising effects, and of water's splashy sounds. Be sure, however, to read the section on water safety: water games can be wet and wild, but they should always end happily.

Drip Drip Drop

PLAYERS 4 or more

EQUIPMENT Bucket of water, sponge or cup

GAME PLAN Beat a friend in a race around the circle (and get a little wet while you're at it!)

HOW TO PLAY

This game is a twist on the standard Duck, Duck, Goose. (See page 91.) Players sit in a circle. One player is chosen to be It and walk around the circle with a wet sponge or a cup of water.

As It walks around, she lets just a little water from the sponge or cup drip on each player, saying "Drip" each time. But then It chooses one lucky (or unlucky) player and wrings out the entire sponge (or empties the cup) on his back, saying, "Drop!"

Once the player has been dropped-on, he and It must race in opposite directions around the circle to the now empty space. The player who gets there last is now It.

The game ends when everyone has had a chance to get soaked or when the game is peaked.

Firefighter Relay

PLAYERS 6 or more

EQUIPMENT 4 buckets, 2 of them filled with water; 2 small plastic, foam or paper cups

GAME PLAN Fill your team's bucket before the other team fills theirs.

HOW TO PLAY

Have players divide into two teams, lining up behind a starting point. At the starting point of the relay, there is a bucket filled with water for each team. At the finish line, there is another empty bucket for each team.

To start the relay, the first player fills a small cup with water and runs to the finish line to pour the water into the empty bucket, then runs back and hands off the empty cup to the next player in line before joining the back of the line. The next player fills up the cup again and runs to the finish, again pouring the water in the bucket.

Inevitably, some water will splash out of the cup in the rush to fill the empty bucket, and one team will end up with more water in their finish-line bucket than the other, making them the winner.

VARIATIONS

Make the relay more challenging by putting a small hole in the bottom of each team's cup!

Wet T-Shirt Relay

PLAYERS 6 or more

EQUIPMENT 4 buckets, 2 of them filled with water; 2 large old T-shirts

GAME PLAN Wear a wet T-shirt, then wring it out to fill your bucket before the other team does.

HOW TO PLAY

Have players divide into two teams, lining up behind a starting point. Much like the Firefighter Relay, at the start point there is a bucket filled with water for each team and an empty bucket for each team at the finish line.

However, rather than filling up a cup with water, participants must take a large, old T-shirt and dunk it in the water, put it on over their clothes, run to the empty bucket, take the T-shirt off and wring the water into the bucket. They then run back to their team and hand off the T-shirt to the next player, who repeats the process.

Once all team members have dunked the T-shirt, worn it, then wrung it out, they should all sit in a straight line and wait for the final measurements. The team with the most water in their finish-line bucket wins.

NOTE We recommend avoiding playing this game with teenage female participants wearing light-colored T-shirts.

Water Limbo

PLAYERS Any number, but best with a large group

EQUIPMENT A water hose

GAME PLAN Limbo under the water.

HOW TO PLAY

One player (or leader) holds on to the hose. Have the rest of the group line up behind the hose.

Turn on the hose at high strength – there should be a jet of water. This will mimic the stick usually used in limbo (see page 105). Hold the stream of water at about shoulder height. Have players bend over backwards (if necessary) and walk underneath the stream of water. If they can walk underneath the stream, they join the back of the line. If they walk into water, they are out.

Once all players have tried to walk under the water at shoulder level, lower it, and repeat the process. Lower the stream each time all players have had a turn. By the end of the game, there will only be one player who can go under the stream (and only one dry player!) That player is the winner.

Water Balloon Toss

PLAYERS 6 or more

EQUIPMENT One water balloon per pair

GAME PLAN Play catch with the water balloon, moving further and further apart.

HOW TO PLAY

Divide the group into pairs. Have players line up facing their partners, facing them, about a foot apart.

Give one player in each pair a water balloon. Count down from three, and have players toss the water balloon to their partner. If they successfully pass it at that distance, they must take one large step back, and the second player tosses the balloon. If they succeed, they take another step back, and so on.

In the unlucky occasion that one of the players tosses the water balloon too hard, or a partner drops the balloon, it's likely to burst all over them, or the ground. When this happens, they are both out. (If the balloon is dropped, but doesn't break, they get another chance to increase their distance.)

The pair that goes furthest without breaking their water balloon wins.

VARIATIONS

Try playing with raw eggs for a gross version of the game.

Wet Potato

PLAYERS 4 or more

EQUIPMENT A pail of water and a sponge

GAME PLAN Pass the "wet potato" around the circle, and avoid getting soaked.

HOW TO PLAY

This is a great variation of the classic "Hot Potato" for one of those sweltering days. Take a sponge and soak it in a pail of water. Pass the sponge around the circle singing: "Wet Potato pass it on, pass it on, pass it on... Wet Potato pass it on, my fair lady-oh." The player who has the sponge on "oh" must squeeze the sponge out on him or herself.

Dunk the sponge in the pail again, and begin passing the sponge around again from where it left off, singing the song.

VARIATIONS

Play without a wet sponge and eliminate the player who is holding it on "oh" to play the classic version, Hot Potato.

Battleship

PLAYERS 10 or more

EQUIPMENT Water balloons, water, clothesline (or volleyball net), large piece of fabric/tarp

GAME PLAN "Sink" as many players on the opposite team as possible — without seeing them.

HOW TO PLAY

Although this game requires a lengthy set-up, it is well worth the wait. Two teams will stand on either side of a clothesline (or volleyball net), with a tarp or fabric hanging down off the line between the teams to obscure their view of the other side. Teams arrange themselves in set positions on their side of the net – and they must not move!

Players will lob water balloons over the net and try to hit a team member on the other side. If hit, they are "sunk" and can enjoy the game from the sidelines, seeing exactly how wild or accurate the players' aim are. The game ends when one team has successfully "sunk" another team.

SWIMMING GAMES

There are plenty of games you can play in the water, either in a swimming pool or lake or river. Besides competitions such as races, obstacle courses and diving contests, you can see who swims the furthest underwater, who can stand on their hands in the water, and who can do the most somersaults without coming up for air.

You may notice that many of our Wet and Wild games are similar to other games for on-land use. This is because most games can be modified to play in the water. Fisherman, for example, is very similar to Octopus (page 125) and Blob Tag (page 119). Use your creativity when modifying games for the water. Keep in mind the swimming abilities of your participants, and whether the game will work with lifejackets on if necessary. Consider

the availability of many water toys, such as pool noodles, kickboards and floating balls.

Some games are better in shallow water. You're lucky if your lake has a soft, sandy bottom. Beach shoes can be a good idea for running around in the shallows if there are clam shells or rocks underfoot. You can make fixed spots such as a ladder, the deep-end rope, the end of the pool, a swimming raft, an anchored canoe or marker buoys a safe home base for games or the start or finish point for a race.

And always make sure your in-the-water games are enjoyable and safe for all, including the weakest swimmers in your group.

Marco Polo

PLAYERS 6 or more

EQUIPMENT None

GAME PLAN Avoid being caught by Marco, whether in the water or as a fish out of water!

HOW TO PLAY

Choose one player to be It. He has to go underwater with eyes closed and, holding his hand above the water, count on his fingers to ten. When he comes up for air, eyes still closed, he yells, "Marco!"

All the other players have to call back, "Polo!" Then It swims toward the sounds of their calls and tries to tag another player with his hand.

Every time he calls out, "Marco," the other players all must call out, "Polo."

The first person tagged becomes It.

VARIATIONS

Fish Out of Water: In this variation of the game, if a player gets out of the pool (or runs out of the lake or gets onto the dock or raft or some other dry place), that player is a Fish out of Water.

If It calls "Fish out of water" while someone is out, that person becomes It. If there is more than one person out, It can choose anyone who is out of water to be the next It.

MODIFICATIONS

If you have participants who cannot swim in the deep end, be sure to mark it off clearly with rope and have all players wear life jackets. We don't want Marco blindly making his way to the deep end!

Colors

PLAYERS 6 or more

EQUIPMENT None

GAME PLAN Swim

HOW TO PLAY

Mark out an area to play in, including a home-free location at one end. Whoever is It stands on the deck of the pool or the shore (or a dock or raft), facing away from all the other players, who are in the water at the same end of the playing area as It.

Each player in the water chooses a color. Then It calls out, "Do you have your colors?" The players answer, "Yes, we do." It then calls out various colors.

When a player's color is called, he has to swim quietly to the edge of the pool, or the shore, or whatever the agreed-upon home-free spot, without being heard.

If It hears the player moving, she can turn around, dive (jump, or climb) into the water and try to catch up to tag him before he reaches the safe spot.

Water Safety

Playing games in the pool is an excellent way to spend supervised time in the water. If children have a chance to play, they will avoid boredom and be less likely to engage in potentially dangerous, boisterous activity.

Before playing water games, it is important to assess the swimming levels of your participants and develop supervision structures to keep your players safe.

Most pools and municipalities have strict guidelines that regulate the age, height, swimming ability, supervision ratios and number of people that can be in the pool at a time. Programs should follow local legal and pool guidelines at all times and should work with pool staff and lifeguards to develop a swim plan that covers everything from getting into the change rooms to dealing with emergencies to leaving the pool.

If you are playing swimming games somewhere other than a life-guarded pool, such as a backyard pool or a lake, do so at your own risk, but keep in mind the following guidelines:

- Swimming with the kids is the best way to supervise them and model appropriate in-pool behavior.

- Ensure that someone in charge has first-aid or lifeguard training and that this person is always present when kids are in the water.
- Designate a shallow end and a deep end.
- Run a "deep-end test" at the beginning of swim sessions. For example, have a child swim the length of the pool without touching the bottom.
- Develop a system for visibly identifying participants who pass the deep-end test.
- Have enough lifejackets (PFDs) for non-swimmers or beginning swimmers so that nobody has to sit out. Consider wearing a lifejacket yourself so that children who do have to wear a lifejacket are following your positive example and are less likely to be picked on.
- Modify water games according to the swimming abilities of your participants.
- Model what appropriate water play looks like, including how to get in and out of the pool safely and the need to respect fellow swimmers by not jumping on them or pretending to drown them.

Sharks and Mermaids

(aka Sharks and Minnows)

PLAYERS 6 or more

EQUIPMENT None

GAME PLAN Avoid being caught by sharks.

HOW TO PLAY

This game is basically Tag in the water. One or two people are chosen to be the Sharks.

The other players (Mermaids or Minnows) are not allowed to leave the water to avoid being tagged, but once they are caught they are out.

You can make a marked spot in the shallow end of the pool, or designate a raft or buoy or spot at the shore's edge your home-free area, where the Mermaids or Minnows may stay for a predetermined (short) amount of time to avoid the Sharks.

MODIFICATIONS

For a more challenging game, have the Sharks swim with one bent arm up and out of the water (mimicking a shark-fin poking out of the water) and Mermaids and Minnows swim with their legs tight together, as if they had a fish-tail instead of two separate legs.

Sun Safety

Part of your responsibility as a program leader is protecting your participants from sun exposure. Here are some tips for preventing sunburns and sunstroke:

Children should bring a hat every day, especially for programs that take place outdoors but even for programs that are only outside for a little bit each day. Encourage participants to wear a hat during water activities. Just because they are wet doesn't mean they are protected against the sun. Leaders should also wear hats!

Make applying sunscreen part of your daily routine. Either have parents apply sunscreen before your participants arrive or apply first thing in the morning, again after lunch, and also after swimming. Taking this time to apply sunscreen yourself will also keep you safe and will serve as an example for your participants.

Play lower intensity games between 10:30 and 2:30, when the sun is extra hot. During peak sun hours, try to spend more time in the shade. Consider purchasing an inexpensive beach umbrella if your site doesn't have shade.

Take frequent water and snack breaks and avoid caffeine and pop, which can dehydrate you.

For other tips, check out our section on Smog Days (page 45).

Water Polo

PLAYERS 6 or more

EQUIPMENT A floating ball (like a beach ball) and two fixed targets

GAME PLAN Score the most goals

HOW TO PLAY

Water Polo is best played in shallow water. Set up fixed targets some distance apart to use as goals, and divide players into two teams.

If you are on a lake and your targets are anchored canoes or other floating objects (for instance, inner tubes), they will move with the wind and the waves. No fair if players move the targets themselves!

Once a player is holding the ball, she cannot move and has to try to score a goal by hitting on or into the target or throw to another player on her team.

Play is continuous, unless the ball goes out of the water, in which case an appointed "goalkeeper" throws it back in. After a goal is scored, the ball is thrown into the middle for a jump ball between the teams.

When playing in a lake, consider establishing side boundaries so you don't go for a swim across the lake.

Still Pond

PLAYERS 4 or more

EQUIPMENT None

GAME PLAN Get to the other side stealthily and make sure It doesn't catch you moving.

HOW TO PLAY

Select one player to be It. She will stand at the opposite end of a pool (or at the end of the designated playing area, like on a raft or dock), facing away and closing her eyes.

Have the other players line up on the opposite end of the playing area. Have It count to ten. While It is counting, the other players begin stealthily sneaking across the pool, as quietly as possible. When It reaches ten, she says, "Still Pond!" and quickly turns around. All the other players must freeze and tread water (or stand if they are in a shallow area).

If It sees anyone still moving forward, she will call them out and send them back to the starting line. For example, if Richard took a chance and went swimming underwater, and did not hear the call for "Still Pond," It may see him moving forward and send him back to the starting point.

It then turns around and counts to ten again, then calls, "Still Pond" to check for anyone moving. The game continues as such until one player makes to the other side of the play area. That person is then the winner, and It for the next round of play.

Musical Kickboards

PLAYERS Best with 6 or more

EQUIPMENT Kickboards (numbering one less than participants), music and player

GAME PLAN When the music stops, find a kickboard!

HOW TO PLAY

Line the kickboards up in a straight line in the water. There should be one less kickboard than players.

Start the music, and have the players swim around the kickboards. Stop the music (at random). All players should grab a kickboard and try to sit on it. This is fun to watch – the kickboards can be quite tricky to clamber onto!

The player left without a kickboard is out, and must leave the water. Remove one kickboard from the water and start the music again, repeating the process until only one kickboard is left. The player who sits on the last kickboard first wins the game.

MODIFICATIONS

If players get too frustrated trying to sit on the kickboard, simply have them grab the kickboard in towards their chest (as if they are hugging it).

NOTE We do not encourage playing a cooperative variation of this (like our cooperative version of Musical Chairs on page 101), as players may push other players under the water in an attempt to sit on the same kickboard.

Fisherman

PLAYERS At least 6, but best with 10 or more

EQUIPMENT None

GAME PLAN Swim from one side to the other without being reeled in by the Fisherman.

HOW TO PLAY

Designate the playing area, with two distinct ends. Choose one player to be the Fisherman. He will stand or tread water in the middle of the playing area. The other players will line up in the water at one end of the play area, they are the fish.

To begin play, the Fisherman will shout "Goin' Fishin'!" and the other players must swim to the other end of the area. While they are swimming, the Fisherman will try to tag the other players.

Any players tagged before reaching the other end must join hands with each other to become the Fisherman's net. They will stand or tread water in the middle of the pool, ready to block or "catch" the fish. The Fisherman is not part of the net, and still free to roam the swim area and catch those who swim around his net.

The game ends when it is peaked, or when one final fish has escaped the Fisherman and his net. She is the winner, and may become the Fisherman for the next round.

Torpedo

PLAYERS Best with 10 or more

EQUIPMENT A few balls that will float (beach balls)

GAME PLAN Make it through the ocean without being hit by an incoming torpedo.

HOW TO PLAY

Divide the group into two equal teams. One team will be "crossing the ocean," and the other team will be launching the torpedoes.

Find a long stretch of water to play in, preferably water deep enough for players to swim and tread water in. This long stretch of water will be the ocean (if it isn't already)!

Explain to the players that they are about to play an old-fashioned game of submarine warfare. Have the first team (say, the Green Team) line up at one end of the ocean. Have the other team (say, the Blue Bombers) stand on both (long) sides of the ocean and give them balls (torpedoes) to throw.

On your signal, the Green Team will swim the length of the ocean between the players on the other team, the Blue Bombers, who are treading water. The swimmers must not swim below water. While the Green Team is swimming, the Blue Bombers can begin to launch their torpedoes, throwing the balls they have at the swimmers. If hit, a swimming player must immediately stop swimming and begin treading water. He or she is now "dead in the water."

Once all Green Team players that are not hit have reached the other side of the ocean, tally the number of players hit by the Blue Bombers' torpedoes. All Green Team players, including those hit in previous rounds, will swim the ocean gauntlet three more times, tallying the number of hits at the end of each turn. Then, the tables turn, and the torpedo-launching team must run the ocean gauntlet, so the Green Team will now be trying to torpedo the Blue Bombers.

Repeat the process. The team with the least number of hits against them at the end of the game wins.

MODIFICATIONS

For beginner swimmers, use lifejackets or choose your water depth so players can stand or swim, depending on their ability. You can also increase or decrease the number of torpedoes.

VARIATIONS

Try playing the on-land version of Torpedo (page 143).

NOTE For safety purposes, it's best to have two leaders supervising during this game. One can ensure that hits are being properly acknowledged and recorded, while the other can focus solely on ensuring player safety in the water.

Stuck in the Mud

PLAYERS 6 or more

EQUIPMENT None

GAME PLAN Don't get stuck in the mud.

HOW TO PLAY

In this game, a sort of aquatic Frozen Tag, one or two players are It and have to capture the others by tagging them. After a player is caught, he has to go to shallower water and stand there, "stuck in the mud," until someone comes along and sets him free by swimming between his legs.

MODIFICATIONS

If there are participants who are uncomfortable swimming underwater (or if participants are wearing lifejackets), have players become unstuck by having another player create a Whirlpool to lift them out. That is, the frozen player must hold out his arms to the side, and the assisting player takes one arm and pushes on it, swimming around the player in a circle (rotating the player using his arm). Once he has spun, he can return to the game.

Acknowledgments

We would like to offer our most grateful thanks to...

...all our favorite campers,

...the people who worked with us for the City of Mississauga Youth Services, especially our partners in crime at CAC and the originals from Camp Totoredaca — long may she live, at least in our memories!

...the Sherikos and Camp Triumph, for leadership games and inspiration,

...Laura Mayne, for her kindergarten games and school stories,

...Rebecca "Palais" Jess and Camp Glen Mhor, for their help with the overnight section,

...the Pollard Drive Gang, for helping make memories of long summer days spent playing outside,

...Papa, for playing the Sleeping Beauty to our Prince Philip, and Grandma, for endless hours of entertainment on the beach.

Thank you to artist Bernice Lum, who has done an amazing job of creating extraordinary characters to play our games, all in a very short time.

Thanks to Chris McCorkindale and Sue Breen of McCorkindale Advertising & Design, for their fabulous design and continuing good cheer under pressure.

Thank you to all at Firefly Books who have helped support us and our book.

Thanks especially to John Denison and Noel Hudson at Boston Mills Press, workmates and dear friends, who kindly said yes in the first place.

A giant-sized thank you to friends and family — you'll see your names in the games — especially Dave and Rosemary, Luke and Drew, Tom and Vicki, Bobby, Shannon and Nolan, Maureen and Peter, Margot and Patrick, and Mom (aka Granny), for cheering us on.

Thank you, Fraser Ash, for sharing camp stories and keeping Laura happy.

Thank you, Rob Hamilton, for sharing school stories and keeping Mary happy.

And in the end, and always, thank you, Sally and Cam.

Bibliography

Brunelle, Lynn. *Camp Out! The Ultimate Kids' Guide from the Backyard to the Backwoods*. New York: Workman, 2007.

Drake, Jane and Ann Love. *The Kids Cottage Games Book*. Toronto, Ontario: Kids Can Press, 1998.

King, Bart. *The Pocket Guide to Games*. Layton, Utah: Gibbs Smith, 2008.

Maguire, Jack. *Hopscotch, Hangman, Hot Potato & Ha Ha Ha*. New York: Prentice Hall Press, 1990.

Strother, Scott. *The Adventurous Book of Outdoor Games*. Naperville, Illinois: Sourcebooks, Inc., 2008.

Wise, Debra. *Great Big Book of Children's Games: Over 450 Indoor and Outdoor Games for Kids*. New York: The Stonesong Press, LLC., McGraw-Hill, 2003.

Index